THE KISS AND THE GHOST
Sylvia Ashton-Warner and New Zealand

Edited by
Alison Jones and Sue Middleton

NZCER PRESS
Wellington 2009

NZCER PRESS

New Zealand Council for Educational Research
PO Box 3237
Wellington
New Zealand

© Alison Jones and Sue Middleton, 2009

ISBN 978-1-877398-47-6

New Zealand edition

International edition published by Sense,
Rotterdam and Taipei

All rights reserved

Designed by Cluster Creative

Printed by Wakefields Digital

Distributed by NZCER Distribution Services
PO Box 3237
Wellington
New Zealand
www.nzcer.org.nz

Contents

CHAPTER 1 Introduction: Sylvia, a New Zealander 5
Alison Jones and Sue Middleton

CHAPTER 2 Creative Teaching Scheme 19
Sylvia Ashton-Warner

CHAPTER 3 Sylvia's place: Ashton-Warner as New Zealand educational theorist 61
Sue Middleton

CHAPTER 4 Far too original: Sylvia Ashton-Warner's novels and her complicated relationship with New Zealand 85
Emily Dobson

CHAPTER 5 Were Sylvia Ashton-Warner's educational ideas really ignored in New Zealand?: The origins of *Teacher* 111
Geraldine McDonald

CHAPTER 6 Publishing Sylvia: C. K. Stead talks to Robert Gottlieb 129
Robert Gottlieb

CHAPTER 7 Teaching with Mere: Sylvia Ashton-Warner's 1973 Canadian university class 145
John Kirkland

| CHAPTER 8 | Sylvia Ashton-Warner and Māori children: "I do not think Sylvia learned much from the kids"
Merimeri Penfold | 161 |

| CHAPTER 9 | Learning without teaching: Sylvia Ashton-Warner's classroom as a seed for kōhanga reo
Iritana Tawhiwhirangi | 171 |

| CHAPTER 10 | Memories of my mother
Elliot Henderson | 179 |

| CHAPTER 11 | Who is Sylvia? The story of a biography
Lynley Hood | 197 |

| Index | | 217 |

CHAPTER 1

Introduction: Sylvia, a New Zealander

Alison Jones and Sue Middleton

Sylvia Ashton-Warner had an intensely ambivalent relationship with the land of her birth. Despite receiving many accolades in New Zealand—including the country's major literary award[1]—she claimed to have been rejected and persecuted, and regularly announced that her educational and literary achievements were unappreciated or insufficiently acknowledged by her compatriots. In her darkest moments, she railed against New Zealand and New Zealanders, even stating in one television interview: "I'm not a New Zealander!"[2] This book makes Sylvia's relationship with New Zealand its central focus.

---

1 Her autobiography *I Passed This Way* won the nonfiction section of the 1980 New Zealand Book Awards.
2 Jack Shallcrass interviewed Sylvia Ashton-Warner on television in 1978. (Barnett, 1978).

Today, Sylvia Ashton-Warner's 11 books—the last of which was published in 1986—are all out of print. When they appeared at the end of the 1950s, her novels *Spinster* and *Incense to Idols* made *Time* magazine's best books lists; in 1963 her teaching scheme, *Teacher*, was favourably reviewed on the front page of the *New York Times Book Review*. But by 2002, C. K. Stead, a leading figure in New Zealand literature, could see no sign in academic or literary circles of "serious interest in her work—a fact all the more puzzling when considered against the background of 1980s feminism and the determined search in universities for neglected women writers" (2002, p. 4). Similarly, New Zealand educationist Alison Jones found that in 2006 amongst "dozens of teacher-trainees, teachers, and teacher-educators in Auckland, most had only a vague idea of who [Sylvia] was" (2006, p. 15).

One of our aims in this book is to introduce Sylvia Ashton-Warner's work to a new generation of readers in literature and education. For those unfamiliar with Sylvia Ashton-Warner's life, we have provided below a short biographical narrative as a guide to the events and places mentioned in this book.

The book's chapters originated as research papers, memoirs or live interviews presented at the International Sylvia Ashton-Warner Centennial Conference—an event held in August 2008 at The University of Auckland's Faculty of Education to mark the centenary of Ashton-Warner's birth. The conference attracted literary scholars, artists, schoolteachers, academic educationists, and biographers—from the USA and Australia as well as New Zealand. As with Sylvia's own writing, the conference crossed genre boundaries between the literary and the pedagogical, and between fiction, biography and theory.

Sylvia Ashton-Warner's refusal to fit any one category may provide a clue to the surprisingly low visibility of her work: It falls between disciplines. Journal articles, reviews and book chapters produced in specialised fields have treated her writing as either educational *or* literary, not as both. But her work itself always defied such simple categorisation: her fiction was autobiographical and her autobiographies were often fictional. Her educational theory was expressed in the form of novels (*Spinster*; *Bell Call*) or as autobiography (*Teacher*; *Spearpoint*). Her noneducational novels (*Greenstone*; *Incense to Idols*; and *Three*) are largely unknown to an education audience, yet these also include elements of her educational thinking.

Lynley Hood's award-winning 1988 biography, *Sylvia! The Biography of Sylvia Ashton-Warner*, meticulously traces her life and her complex personality, but it does not interrogate Sylvia's educational or literary contributions, or the relations between the two. So a second objective of this book, and of the conference in which it originated, is to pull together some of the strands of Sylvia Ashton-Warner's writing by examining it within the context of its production.

Other works

Portrayals of Sylvia Ashton-Warner's life are scattered through visual and print media.[3] Her life has been the subject of New Zealand radio and television interviews and documentaries, and two fictionalised films.[4] Her own self-portrayals are in two autobiographies (*Myself*, 1967, and *I Passed This Way*, first published in 1979 by Knopf), as well as being woven into all her novels. Lynley Hood's excellent biography retraced the convoluted paths of Sylvia's autobiographical narratives, interrogated their historical accuracy, speculated on their psychological underpinnings and reviewed her work's reception.

---

3   The best source of references to textual portrayals of Sylvia's life is in Hood (1988, p. 256–258). Television programmes include *Three New Zealanders: Sylvia Ashton-Warner* (Barnett, 1978) (a copy is held by the New Zealand Film Archive) and an interview on *Kaleidoscope* (Interview, 1980).
4   One film was *Two Loves* (Walter & Maddow, 1961), based on her first novel *Spinster*, and starring Shirley MacLaine. The other was the 1985 New Zealand-produced *Sylvia* (Firth & Fairfax) based on her autobiographical writing.

Hood also published a personal account of her research process, *Who is Sylvia? The Diary of a Biography* (1990).

Aside from biography and autobiography, only two full-length books have been written about Sylvia Ashton-Warner: both from an educational perspective, and both from outside New Zealand. Sydney Gurewitz Clemens' 1996 book, *Pay Attention to the Children: Lessons for Teachers and Parents from Sylvia Ashton-Warner* is an American handbook for teachers.[5] A 2006 collection is *Provocations: Sylvia Ashton-Warner and Excitability in Education* edited by a Canadian (Judith Robertson) and an Australian (Cathryn McConaghy). Three chapters in that collection focus explicitly on Ashton-Warner's New Zealand context: Sue Middleton places Ashton-Warner's theoretical writing on education in wider sites of educational writing and publishing in New Zealand; Alison Jones explores the philosophy and practice of her pedagogy which, considered in the light of today's social anxieties in New Zealand about children, make Ashton-Warner's teaching methods both compelling *and* dangerous for contemporary educators; and Tess Moeke-Maxwell offers a reading of the biracial character Huia in Ashton-Warner's novel, *Greenstone*.

While *Pay Attention* was a practical guide, aimed at American classroom teachers, *Provocations* was more theoretical, for academic readers. In their introduction to *Provocations*, McConaghy and Robertson (2006) noted a shift in focus "from subject to theory" in studies of Ashton-Warner. Sylvia herself rejected classification as teacher or theorist. Describing herself as an artist rather than a teacher, she claimed to read "nothing on teaching" or education and expressed a dislike of academic educational theory's "unintelligible multisyllabic jargon" (1979/1980, p. 471). Refusing to acknowledge other educationists' contributions to her ideas, she claimed

---

5   Clemens provided for the conference a DVD of her lecture entitled "Sylvia Ashton-Warner goes to Reggio Emilia".

intellectual autonomy: "I am my own university, I my own Professor [sic]" (1979/1980, p. 354).

McConaghy and Robertson's text focused on what they termed "the psychic" rather than on the "historical and sociospatial conditions" (2006, p. 5) informing Sylvia's work and commentaries on it. Sylvia's "sociospatial conditions" have long bewildered foreign commentators who, from a distance, allow themselves to see Sylvia's New Zealand as suffocating. American teacher Sydney Gurewitz Clemens wrote (1996, p. 23): "Astonishingly, it was in conventional, dutiful New Zealand that Sylvia Ashton-Warner began a lifelong habit of listening to her inner voice, embarking on the journey toward abundant life in 1940!" Similarly, speaking from France, another critic argued: "In the fifties her ideas were revolutionary. At a time when the curriculum was binding and the individuality of the pupils was largely ignored, her theories disturbed the establishment" (Durix, interviewed in Connor, Radford, & Robertson, 2006, p. 158). Indeed, there are repeated assertions that Sylvia's educational theory was "in confrontation … with the time and place in which she lived" (Clemens, 1996, p. 28).

Less than strictly accurate

Our book takes a critical position with regard to this depiction of Sylvia's environment. The crushing conformity was something she herself painted with flair, but it was a less-than-strictly-accurate portrayal of New Zealand educational conditions, which in fact reflected the international Progressive movement in encouraging children to express (up to a point) their own lives and passions. Indeed, it could be argued that the New Zealand education establishment's attention to Sylvia the teacher arose from its interest in how to put these ideas into practice.

But Ashton-Warner repeatedly claimed that New Zealand teachers, education officials and publishers had rejected her educational theory, pedagogical techniques and her educational writing. Although conclusively disputed by the research of Lynley Hood and others, impressions of Sylvia's exclusion and rejection continue to be perpetuated in New Zealand and overseas. Accordingly, in Chapter 2 we have reprinted Ashton-Warner's original 1950s teaching-scheme articles from *National Education* (the magazine of the national primary teachers' union, the New Zealand Educational Institute, or NZEI) published some years before *Spinster* and *Teacher*. Our reprinting makes the original version of her teaching scheme readily available—as it was when it first appeared in 1956, and welcomed by the educational establishment. Lynley Hood records that

> since [Sylvia's teaching scheme's] serialised appearance in 1956 [in *National Education*], training-college lecturers had been recommending it to students, and inspectors had been recommending it to teachers. And since the advent of *Spinster*, requests for more information on the key vocabulary had streamed in. (1988, p. 170)

This collection

Our book's title, *The Kiss and the Ghost*, refers to Sylvia Ashton-Warner's famous key vocabulary reading scheme. On the basis of her work with Māori children in rural and often remote Native Schools[6] in the post-war years of the 1940s and early 1950s, she argued that literacy was best achieved when children found words for their experiences of fear and sex, the two great Freudian drives. The most powerful words, she argued, were *kiss* (a sex word) and *ghost* (a fear word). Venting the fear/destructive drive through captions (the child's key vocabulary) and other expressive arts could, she believed, prevent violence and war. This was the theory she elaborated in her novel *Spinster*, and in her descriptions of her work in *Teacher*.

---

6 For information about the New Zealand Native Schools, see Barrington (2008); Simon (1998); Simon & Tuhiwai Smith (2001).

The contributors to this collection position Sylvia Ashton-Warner as an educational and literary figure in the New Zealand landscapes in which she lived, taught, thought, loved and wrote for most of her life. Sylvia's eldest son, Elliot Henderson, recalls vividly his mother in various rural settings; her biographer Lynley Hood confesses to personal struggles with writing a biography of such a contradictory and enigmatic character; and John Kirkland, Sylvia's then assistant, provides insights into Sylvia's teacher-training methods at Simon Fraser University in Canada.

Merimeri Penfold and Iritana Tawhiwhirangi are Māori teachers who worked briefly alongside Sylvia in Waiomatatini in the 1940s. They provide a sense of how Sylvia was understood within Māori communities. Penfold recalls her own radical teaching that stimulated Māori children to speak their own language in the classroom, a practice actively rejected by the New Zealand educational establishment. Tawhiwhirangi provides insight into why Sylvia and other teachers taught in English at that time, and—interestingly—names Sylvia as "a seed" for the kōhanga reo movement, a preschool programme in Māori language.

Literary scholar Emily Dobson examines Ashton-Warner's status within New Zealand literature by mapping the development of critical responses to her work, and also provides a literary critique of two of Sylvia Ashton-Warner's novels, *Incense to Idols* and *Bell Call*. Geraldine McDonald carries out forensic work on the production of Sylvia's *National Education* articles in New Zealand (reprinted in Chapter 2) and their reappearance in *Teacher* in the United States. Sue Middleton explores the ideas and texts available to Sylvia in the environment in which she lived, taught, studied and wrote. Middleton argues that as a teacher, educational writer and theorist, Sylvia Ashton-Warner grew *in*, and not in spite of, New Zealand.

While the contributions by New Zealand writers are based on memories of Sylvia Ashton-Warner, or research carried out in New

Zealand, others who have engaged with her from afar document the impressions Sylvia created of this country elsewhere. Our collection includes a transcript of the video-link discussion at the conference between C. K. Stead (New Zealand novelist, poet, critic and scholar) and the New York-based publisher of *Teacher* and almost all of Sylvia's books, Robert Gottlieb,[7] who had been unaware that Sylvia had previously been published in New Zealand.

Short biography

Sylvia Warner was born in Stratford, Taranaki, New Zealand, on 17 December 1908. Her father, crippled with an arthritic condition, was unable to provide for the family, so, unusually for the time, her mother supported her husband and 10 children by teaching in small, often sole-charge, rural schools. The family moved frequently. Often taught by her authoritarian mother, Sylvia attended 10 different primary schools. After attending secondary school in Masterton, she became a pupil teacher at Wellington South School (1926–7). While at Auckland Teachers' Training College (1928–9) she met her future husband, fellow student Keith Henderson. The couple married on 23 August 1931. In their first years of marriage, Keith taught sole-charge schools in Taranaki, and Sylvia gave birth to three children—Jasmine in 1935, Elliot in 1937 and Ashton in 1938. In his chapter in this volume, Elliot Henderson recollects childhood memories of life with Sylvia.

At Sylvia's suggestion, she and Keith applied to teach in what was at the time referred to as the Native School system, and they took up their first position in 1938 at Horoera Native School, on the remote East Cape, eight miles from the nearest village, Te Araroa. At this

---

7   Gottlieb, at Simon and Schuster and later at Knopf and elsewhere, went on to invent the title Catch-22 and edit Toni Morrison's work, Chaim Potok's The Chosen, John Cheever's posthumous collections, and Bill Clinton's autobiography, to name a few of his achievements.

time Sylvia experienced what was described as a severe "nervous breakdown". Her Wellington neurologist, Dr Allen, introduced Sylvia to psychoanalytic theory and encouraged her to write.

In 1941, the family moved to Pipiriki Native School, up the Whanganui River valley, in the western-central North Island. Sylvia became a serious writer (see Middleton, Chapter 3). The diary she kept during those years would later be published as *Myself*. From 1945 to 1948, the couple taught at another east coast school at Waiomatatini (see Penfold and Tawhiwhirangi, in Chapters 8 and 9). It was here that Sylvia began publishing short stories. Her first major publications were produced when she was further down the east coast at Fernhill School, Ōmahu, near Hastings (from 1949 to 1957), including the first, serialised, New Zealand version of her teaching scheme, published under the name "Sylvia" (reprinted in Chapter 2. See also McDonald, Chapter 5). The pen name Sylvia Ashton-Warner first appeared in 1958, on the original, British (Secker & Warburg), edition of her novel *Spinster*.

When Keith was appointed headmaster of Bethlehem Maori School near Tauranga in 1957, Sylvia began to work full-time on her writing—and established a relationship with New York publisher Robert Gottlieb (which Gottlieb discusses in Chapter 6).

After Keith Henderson died on 7 January 1969, Sylvia embarked on her first overseas travel. A period in London with her son Elliot inspired her final novel, *Three*. In late 1970 she took up an invitation to establish a community school at Aspen, Colorado, where she spent one year. Her final book about education, *Spearpoint: 'Teacher' in America*, was her account of this experience. During 1972–3, Sylvia was employed at Vancouver's Simon Fraser University, where she ran courses on her teaching methods. John Kirkland in Chapter 7 describes his experiences as an assistant in this programme. Sylvia's book of short stories *O Children of the World* (1974) was written during this time away, and work was started on her autobiography *I Passed This Way*.

Sylvia returned to Tauranga, where she completed *I Passed This Way* (1979/1980) and advised on the production of the film, *Sylvia*. In Chapter 11 Hood discusses her encounters with Sylvia during these years, as she researched her biography (Hood, 1988, 1990[8]). Sylvia Ashton-Warner died in Tauranga on 27 April 1984.

Alison Jones and Sue Middleton
December 2008

References

Ashton-Warner, S. (1958). *Spinster*. London: Secker & Warburg.

Ashton-Warner, S. (1960). *Incense to idols*. London: Secker & Warburg.

Ashton-Warner, S. (1963). *Teacher*. New York: Simon & Schuster.

Ashton-Warner, S. (1964). *Bell call*. New York: Simon & Schuster.

Ashton-Warner, S. (1966). *Greenstone*. New York: Simon & Schuster.

Ashton-Warner, S. (1967). *Myself*. New York: Simon & Schuster.

Ashton-Warner, S. (1970). *Three*. New York: Knopf.

Ashton-Warner, S. (1972). *Spearpoint: 'Teacher' in America*. New York: Knopf.

Ashton-Warner, S. (1974). *O children of the world*. Vancouver: First Person Press.

Ashton-Warner, S. (1979/1980). *I passed this way*. Wellington: A. H & A. W. Reed (First published in 1979, New York: Knopf).

Ashton-Warner, S. (1986). *Stories from the river*. Auckland: Hodder & Stoughton.

Barnett, J. (Producer). (1978). *Three New Zealanders: Sylvia Ashton-Warner* [Television programme]. Wellington: Endeavour Films.

Barrington, J. (2008). *Separate but equal?: Māori schools and the Crown, 1867–1969*. Wellington: Victoria University Press.

---

[8] 2008 editions of Lynley Hood's books about Sylvia Ashton-Warner were launched at the conference, published by Penguin and Longacre respectively.

Clemens, S. (1996). *Pay attention to the children: Lessons for teachers and parents from Sylvia Ashton-Warner*. Napa, CA: Rattle OK Publications.

Connor, K., Radford, L., & Robertson, J. (2006). Reading in(to) Sylvia: Interviews on Sylvia Ashton-Warner's influence. In J. Robertson & C. McConaghy (Eds.), *Provocations: Sylvia Ashton-Warner and excitability in education* (pp. 155–193). New York: Peter Lang.

Firth, M. (Director) & Fairfax, F. (Writer). (1985). *Sylvia* [Motion picture]. New Zealand: Cinepro.

Hood, L. (1988). *Sylvia! The biography of Sylvia Ashton-Warner*. Auckland: Viking.

Hood, L. (1990). *Who is Sylvia? The diary of a biography*. Dunedin: John McIndoe.

[Interview]. (1980, 24 March). In *Kaleidoscope* [Television series]. Auckland: Television New Zealand.

Jones, A. (2006). Sex, fear and pedagogy: Sylvia Ashton-Warner's infant room. In J. Robertson & C. McConaghy (Eds.), *Provocations: Sylvia Ashton-Warner and excitability in education* (pp. 15–32). New York: Peter Lang.

McConaghy, C., & Robertson, J. (2006). Sylvia Ashton-Warner: Reading provocatively from subject to theory. In J. Robertson & C. McConaghy (Eds.), *Provocations: Sylvia Ashton-Warner and excitability in education* (pp. 1–14). New York: Peter Lang.

Middleton, S. (2006). "I my own professor": Ashton-Warner as New Zealand educational theorist 1940–1960. In J. Robertson & C. McConaghy (Eds.), *Provocations: Sylvia Ashton-Warner and excitability in education* (pp. 37–55). New York: Peter Lang.

Moeke-Maxwell, T. (2006). InSide/OutSide cultural hybridity: *Greenstone* as narrative provocateur. In J. Robertson & C. McConaghy (Eds.), *Provocations: Sylvia Ashton-Warner and excitability in education* (pp. 95–117). New York: Peter Lang.

Robertson, J., & McConaghy, C. (Eds.). (2006). *Provocations: Sylvia Ashton-Warner and excitability in education*. New York: Peter Lang.

Simon, J. (Ed.). (1998) *Ngā kura Māori: The native schools system*. Auckland: Auckland University Press.

Simon J., & Tuhiwai Smith, L. (Eds.). (2001). *A civilising mission? Perceptions and representations of the Native Schools system.* Auckland: Auckland University Press.

Stead, C. K. (2002). *Kin of place: Essays on 20 New Zealand writers.* Auckland: Auckland University Press.

Sylvia (1955, December 1). No. 1: Organic reading and the key vocabulary. *National Education, 406,* 392–393.

Sylvia (1956, February 1). No. 2: Private key vocabularies. *National Education, 407,* 10–12.

Sylvia (1956, March 1). No. 3: Organic writing. *National Education, 408,* 54–55.

Sylvia (1956, April 3). No. 4: Organic reading. *National Education, 409,* 97–98.

Sylvia (1956, May 1). Organic reading is not new. *National Education, 410,* 141.

Sylvia (1956, August 1). Nature study and number: The golden section. *National Education, 413,* 248–251.

Sylvia (1956, September 3). Organic teaching: The unlived life. *National Education, 414,* 294–295.

Sylvia (1956, October 1). Tone. *National Education, 415,* 342–3.

Walters, C. (Director), & Maddow, B. (Writer). (1961). *Two loves* [Motion picture]. United States: Julian Blaustein Productions.

Authors

Alison Jones is a professor of education at The University of Auckland. Her mother's friendship with Sylvia, and her interest in Pākehā involvement in Māori education, has led her attention to Sylvia Ashton-Warner. Her chapter in *Provocations: Sylvia Ashton-Warner and Excitability in Education* (edited by J. Robertson & C. McConaghy) critiques romanticized claims about the child's "native imagery". She is author of several books and articles in the general field of cultural studies in education in New Zealand.
Email: a.jones@auckland.ac.nz

Sue Middleton is a professor of education at the University of Waikato. She has an interest in the lives and works of New Zealand educational theorists; in particular, women teachers who were also writers (such as Sylvia Ashton-Warner), and how their educational ideas were enabled and constrained by their historical circumstances. Her books include: *Disciplining Sexuality: Foucault, Life-histories and Education; Teachers Talk Teaching 1915–1995: Early Childhood, Schools, and Teachers' Colleges; Women and Education in Aotearoa.*
Email: educ_mid@waikato.ac.nz

CHAPTER 2

Creative Teaching Scheme

Sylvia Ashton-Warner

Sylvia Ashton-Warner said she could not get her Creative Teaching Scheme published in New Zealand. *National Education* (the journal of the NZEI, the primary teachers' association[1]) did in fact publish her scheme, to acclaim, in eight instalments, in 1955–56. As described by Hood (1988) and McDonald (see Chapter 5, this volume), the instalments were structured and edited by Russell Bond. Each are by Sylvia. We reprint the eight articles here, including their grammatical errors.

---

1   The name of the NZEI journal is now *Rourou*. Thanks to *Rourou's* editor Noel O'Hare for his support for this reprinting.

The Māori Infant Room: Organic Reading and the Key Vocabulary.
National Education, 1 December 1955, pp. 392–393

The method of teaching any subject in a Māori infant room may be seen as a plank in a bridge from one culture to another, from which, either that this bridge is strengthened may a Māori in after life succeed socially [*sic*].

This transition of Māori children is often unsuccessful. At this tender age a wrench occurs from one culture to another, from which, either manifestly or subconsciously, not all recover. And I think that this circumstance has some little bearing on the number of Māoris who, although well educated, seem neurotic, and on the number who retreat to the mat.

Another more obvious cause of the social failure of Māoris is the delay in the infant room. Owing to this delay, which is due to language as well as to the imposition of a culture, many children arrive at the secondary school stage too old to fit in with the European group and they lose heart to continue. From here, being too young and unskilled to do a competent job, some fall in and out of trouble, by European standards become failures, and by the time they have grown up have lost the last and most precious of their inheritances, their social stability.

With this in mind, therefore, I see any subject whatever in a Māori infant room as a plank in the bridge from the Māori to the European. In particular, reading.

So, in preparing reading for a Māori infant room, a teacher tries to bridge the division between the races and to jettison the excess time.

The Key to vocabulary

Children have two visions, the inner and the outer. Of the two the inner vision is the brighter.

I hear that in other infant-rooms widespread illustration is used to introduce the reading vocabulary to a five-year-old, a vocabulary chosen by adult educationists. I use pictures, too, to introduce the reading vocabulary but they are pictures of the inner vision and the captions are chosen by the children themselves. True, the picture of the outer, adult chosen pictures can be meaningful and delightful to children; but it is the captions of the mind pictures that have the power and the light. For whereas the illustrations perceived by the outer eye cannot be other than interesting, the illustrations seen by the inner eye are organic and it is the captioning of these that I call "the key vocabulary."

I see the mind of a five-year-old as a volcano with two vents; destructiveness and creativeness. And I see that to the extent that we widen the creative channel we atrophy the destructive one. And it seems to me that since these words of the key vocabulary are no less than the captions of the dynamic life itself, they course out through the creative channel, making their contribution to the drying up of the destructive vent. From all of which I am constrained to see it as creative reading and to teach it among the arts.

Mohi, I ask a new five, an undisciplined Māori, what word do you want?

Jet!

I smile and write it on strong little card and give it to him. What is it again?

Jet!

You can bring it back in the morning. What do you want, Gay?

Gaynor is the classic over-disciplined, bullied victim of the respectable mother.

House, she whispers. So I write that, too, and give it into her eager hand.

What do you want, Joseph? Joseph is a violent Māori.

Bomb! Bomb! I want bomb!

So Joseph gets his word bomb and challenges anyone to take it from him.

And so on through the rest of them. They ask for a new word each morning and never have I to repeat to them what it is. And if you saw the condition of these tough little cards the next morning you'd know why they need to be tough cards rather than paper.

When each has the nucleur of a vocabulary and I know they are at peace with me I show them the word "frightened" and at once all together they burst out with what they are frightened of. Nearly all the Māoris say "the Ghost!" a matter which has a racial and cultural origin, while the Europeans name some animal they have never seen, "tiger" or "alligator," using it symbolically for the unnameable fear that we all have.

I not frightened of anysing! shouts my future murderer, Joseph.

Aren't you?

No, I stick my knife into it all!

What will you stick your knife into?

I stick my knife into the tigers!

"Tigers" is usually a word from the European children but here is a Māori with it. So I give him "tigers" and never have I to repeat the word to him, and in the morning the little card shows the dirt and disrepair of passionate usage.

Come in, cry the children to a knock at the door, but as no one does come in we all go out. And here we find in the porch, humble with natural dignity, a barefooted, tattooed Māori woman.

I see my little Joseph? She says.

Is Joseph your little boy?

I bring him up. Now he five. I bring him home to his real family for school eh. I see my little boy?

The children willingly produce Joseph and here we have in the porch, within a ring of sympathetic brown and blue eyes, a reunion.

Where did you bring him up? I ask over the many heads.

Way back on those hill. All by heeself. You remember your ol' Mummy? she begs Joseph.

I see.

Later, standing watching Joseph grinding his chalk to dust on his blackboard as usual, I do see. Whom do you want Joseph? Your old Mummy or your new Mummy?

My old Mummy.

What do your brothers do?

They all hits me.

"Old Mummy" and "New Mummy" and "hit" and "brothers" and others are all one-look words added to his vocabulary, and now and again I see some shape breaking though the chalk-ravage. And I wish I could make a good story of it and say he is no longer violent …

Who's that crying! I accuse, lifting my nose like an old war-horse.

Joseph he is breaking Gaynor's neck.

So the good story, I say to my junior, must stand by for a while. But I can say he is picking up his words now. Fast.

But I couldn't get any words from Rangi in six months.

What are you frightened of, Rangi?

Police.

Why?

Police they takes me to gaol and cuts me up with a butcher knife.

What Rangi's home like. I ask the Head.

His father runs a gambling den at the hotel.

I see.

Gaol, butcher knife, kill, police, were the one-look words upon which Rangi burst into reading. He's a most expressive reader now.

Dennis is a victim of the respectable, money-making, well dressed mother, who thrashes him, and at five he has already had his first nervous breakdown. I'm not frightened of anything! he cries.

Is Dennis afraid of anything? I asked his young pretty mother in her big car.

Dennis? He won't even let the chickens come near him.

Did you have a dream? I asked Dennis after his afternoon rest.

Yes I did.

Well then … where's some chalk and a blackboard?

Later when I walked that way there was a dreadful brown ghost with purple eyes facing a red alligator on a roadway. I know I have failed with Dennis. I've never had his fear-words. His mother has defeated me. During the morning output period—when everyone else is painting, claying, dancing, quarrelling, singing, drawing, taking, writing or building—Dennis is picking up my things from the floor and straightening the mats, and the picture I have of his life waiting for him, another neurotic, pursued by the fear unnameable, is not one of comfort.

Wiki learnt nothing for many months until one night I heard for myself a violent physical fight between her mother and father, with the awakened children screaming. The next day she recognised the words, "hit," "crack," "fight," "scrubbing brush," "Mummy and Daddy" after one look and broke at once into reading and I wish you could hear Wiki read now.

Mare resisted any kind of vocabulary until one morning when the little ones were all talking at once about what they were frightened of he let go, "I shoot the bulldog!" Gaynor's fear was a dog, too. Do we realise just how afraid small children are of dogs?

But I have some dirty, thoroughly-spoilt children next door who are never held up with fear. Their key vocabulary runs from "Daddy" and "kiss" through words like "truck" "hill" and "Mummy" to "love" and "train." How glorious are the dirty spoilt children.

Out press these words, grouping themselves in their own wild order. All boys wanting words of locomotion, aeroplane, tractor, jet, and the girls the words of domesticity, house, Mummy, doll. Then the fear words, ghost, tiger, skellington, alligator, bulldog, wild piggy, police. The sex words, kiss, love, touch, haka. The key words carrying their own illustration in the mind, vivid and powerful pictures which none of us could possibly draw for them—since in the first place we can't see them and secondly because they are so alive with an organic life that the external pictorial representation of them is beyond the frontiers of possibility. We can do no more than supply the captions.

Out push these words. The tendency is for them to gather force once the fears are said, but there are so many variations on character. Even more so in this span of life where personality has not yet been moulded into the general New Zealand pattern by the one imposed vocabulary for all. They are more than captions. They are even more than sentences. They are whole stories at times. They are actually schematic reading on a level with schematic drawing. I know because they tell them to me.

Out flow these captions. It's a lovely flowing. I see the creative channel swelling and undulating like an artery with blood pumping through. And as it settles, just like any other organic arrangement of nature it spreads out into an harmonious pattern; the fear-words dominating the design, a few sex words, the person interest, and the temper of the century. Daddy, Mummy, ghost, bomb, kiss, brothers, butcher-knife, gaol, love, dance, cry, fight, hat, bulldog, touch, will piggy [*sic*]… if you were a child which vocabulary would you prefer? Your own or the one at present in the New Zealand infant rooms?

Come John come. Look John look. Come and look. See the boats? The vocabulary of the upper English middle-class, two dimensional and respectable?

Out pelt these captions; these one-word accounts of the pictures within. Is it art? Is it creation? Is it reading? I know that it is integral. It is organic. And it is the most vital and the most sure reading vocabulary a child can build. It is the key that unlocks the mind and releases the tongue. It is the key that opens the door upon a love of reading. It is the organic foundation of a life-time of books. It is the key that I use daily with my fives, along with the clay and the paint and amid the singing and quarrelling.

It is the key whose turning preserves intact for a little longer the true personality. It's the key vocabulary.

* This article is reprinted from the December, 1952, issue of *"Here and Now."*

The Māori Infant Room: No. 2: Private Key Vocabularies. *National Education*, 1 February 1956, pp. 10–12

In my first article I said that the illustrations chosen by adults to introduce the reading vocabulary could be meaningful and delightful, but that it was the pictures of the inner vision and the captions chosen by the children themselves that had the power and the light. However, there is still the odd child who is too emotionally disturbed to caption the inner picture at all.

Rangi, a backward Māori, after learning eight Māori nouns, stalled on the words "come, look, and" for weeks until it occurred to me to ask him what he was frightened of. He said he was frightened of the police. Asked why, he replied that the police would take him to gaol in the fire-engine, cut him up with a butcher knife, kill him and hang up what was left of him. When I told the head about this, he said that Rangi's father ran a gambling den down at the hotel to keep the home going and himself in beer and that the whole family lived in the shadow of the police and that the children had probably been threatened in order not to tell.

When I gave these words to Rangi—police, butcher-knife, kill, gaol, hang and fire-engine, they proved themselves to be what I call one-look words, by which I mean he knew them for good after one look. Whereas he had spent four months on come, look, and, he spent four minutes on these. So from these I made him reading cards and at last Rangi was a reader.

Wiki, who comes from a clever family, and whose mother and father fight bitterly and physically and often, breaking out in the night and alarming the children who wake and scream (I've heard all of this myself), after learning two words in six months burst into reading on Daddy, Mummie, Wiki, fight, yell, hit, crack, frightened, broom. It is an opportune moment to observe the emotional distance of these private key vocabularies from the opening words of the "Janet and John" book:

> Janet John come look and see the boats little dog run here down up

There are always these special cases on the handling of which depends the child's start in school. No time is too long spent talking to a child to find out his key words, the key that unlocks himself for in them is the secret of reading, the realisation that words can have intense meaning. Words having no emotional significance to him, no instinctive meaning, could be an imposition, doing him more harm than not teaching him at all. They may teach him that words mean nothing and that reading is undesirable.

The fact that certain words can be surmounted by the average reader does not prove them. That's the red herring. The weight of a word is proved by the backward reader. And there are many backward Māori readers. And to begin them on such bloodless words as come, look, and . . . provokes one to experiment.

The key vocabulary of a Māori infant room, outside the common vocabulary of fear and sex, changes all the time like anything else alive, but here is the current key vocabulary running through the infant room this week, from the newcomers. All Māoris.

Mohi: Ghost jet jeep skellington bike aeroplane sausage porridge egg car beer jersey kiss

Joe Joe: King of the Rocket Men, Indian Phantom Superman

Gilbert: frog walnut truck King of the Rocket Men jet jeep beer tractor bomb horse.

Moreen: Mummie Daddy Tape (dog) lambie Kuia kiss

Penny: Daddy Mummie house plane car

Rongo: peanut cake ghost bed kiss socks

Phillip: train boxing truck pea rifle

Phyllis: beer pudding bus darling kiss ghost

The words when I print them on big cards fill them with smiles and excitement.

Words over the past two years, however, from the Māori newcomers group themselves as follows: all one-look words: to the particular child.

Fear (the strongest): Mummie Daddy ghost frightened skellington wild piggie police spider dog gaol bull kill butcher-knife yell hit crack fight thunder alligator cry . . . .

Sex: kiss love haka dance darling together Me-and-you sing . . .

Locomotion: jet jeep aeroplane train car truck trailer bus . . .

Others: house school socks frog walnut peanut porridge pictures beer.

Emerging from two years of observation, however, are the two most powerful words in the infant room under any circumstance:

ghost kiss

representing in their own way, possibly, the two main instincts. Any child, brown or white, on the first day, remembers these words from One-Look.

Yet do I include them in a first reading book? There's no end to courage but there is an end to the strength required to swim against the current. For here is the opening vocabulary of Janet and John:

> Janet John come look and see the boats little dog run here down up aeroplane my one kitten I two three play jump can go horse ride.

Between these and the key vocabulary is there any emotional difference? There is all the difference between something that comes through the creative vent and something that approaches from the outside. Which is the difference between the organic vocabulary and the inorganic.

The mechanics of teaching the key vocabulary

I take the key vocabulary in the morning output period when the energy is at its highest, since it is a creative activity, and I believe that the creative activities are more important than anything else. It's where I place all the media of creativeness, between nine and ten-thirty.

I take in the minute they come in before they touch any other medium, because I don't like to interrupt them later when they are deep in blocks of clay. Also I want to catch the first freshness.

The preparation is modest enough. A number of cards at hand, about a foot long and five inches wide, of cheap drawing paper quality, and a big black crayon. And a cardboard cover a size or two larger than the cards. And their old cards tipped out on the mat.

I call a child to me and ask her what she wants. She may ask for "socks" and I print it largely on a card with her name written quickly in the corner for my own use. She watches me print the word and says it as I print, then I give it to her to take back to the mat and I trace the characters with her finger and finally replace it in the cover nearby. I call them one by one until each child has a new word.

These self-chosen words mount up and are kept in a box. Each morning before they came in I tip them out on the mat so that when they run in from assembly they make straight for them to find their own, not without quarrelling and concentration and satisfaction. When they have collected their own they choose a mate and sit together and hear each other their own and the other's words. All this, of course, takes time and involves noise and movement and personal relations and actual reading, and above all communication, one with another; the vital thing so often cut off in a school room. And it is while they are teaching each other, far more effectively than I could teach them myself, that I call each one to me separately to get his new word for the day.

She comes to me with her old words and says them as she puts them back in the box; but the ones she doesn't remember I take from her and destroy because the word has failed as a one-look word and cannot have been of much importance to her. And it is the words that are important to her that I am after. For it is from these words that she first realises that reading can be of intense meaning to herself. So the only words she keeps are those that have come from deep within herself and have to be told only once.

It is at this stage that I say, "What are you going to have?" Sometimes she will have it all bubbling hot, "Toast!" and sometimes she will twist her foot and think and then I suspect the validity of it when she looks about and says "windows." And as often as not, later in the day when these words are checked she won't recognise it. So I engage her in conversation until I find out that she sleeps with Maude, or that Daddy has gone to the shearing shed. And I ask her again and may get "shed" or "Maude," which might well prove valid. But they're not often like this and I print the asked for word on the card while she watches me and says it while I print. Then I give it to her to take back to the mat and trace it with her finger before putting it back in the cover.

I make mistakes over the choice of these words on occasion. It takes me a little while to assess the character of each newcomer. For the variety of character on the five-year-old level is as legion as nature itself. And there are pitfalls like copying, mood, repression and crippling fears which block the organic expulsion of a word. But you get to know all these after a while an sometimes later on, a regular flow of organic words which are captions to the pictures of the mind.

It may sound hard, but it's the easiest way I have ever begun reading. There's no driving to it. I don't teach at all. There is no work to put up on the blackboard, no charts to make and no force to marshal them into a teachable and attentive group. The teaching is done between themselves, mixed up with all the natural concomitants of relationship. I just make sure of my cards nearby and my big black crayon and look forward to the game with myself of seeing how nearly I hit the mark. And the revelation of character is a thing that no one can ever find boring.

After the morning interval during what I call my intake period the new words of the morning come out of the cover and I check to see which are remembered. They mostly are but the ones that are not are taken away and old ones take their place, so that when they attempt to write them they are writing words that carry with them an inner picture and are of organic origin.

Then they go back in the box to be tipped out on the mat the next morning. When there is a small group of beginners, the number of the known words mounting up in the box need have no limit, but in direct ratio to the growing size of the group the number of words kept per child diminishes until with a group of twelve to twenty it is not feasible to keep more than the last two for each child.

Notes

A minimum of forty personal words before passing on into the next group. But promotion with me depends not on the amount of intake but the rate of intake.

I make the cards from large sheets of cheap drawing paper. If a child copies a word of another she won't remember it the next time she meets it.

A new word every week, however shy or speechless or dull the newcomer. In time she will see that the differing marks on this paper mean important and different things.

What I call teaching each other: One holds up the card with "socks" to the other and says, "What's that?" If the other doesn't know, the first one tells him.

After the key vocabulary first thing in the morning they go on to other media of expression.

The Māori Infant Room: No. 3: Organic Writing. *National Education*, 1 March 1956, pp. 54–55

"Life as a whole is too complicated to teach to children. The minute it is cut up they can understand it, but you are liable to kill it in cutting it up."
—C. E. Beeby

Creative writing follows on from the key vocabulary. Whereas the key vocabulary is a one-word caption of the inner world, creative writing is a sentence-length or story-length caption. From schematic writing they progress towards the representational.

The creative writing of fives begins with their attempt to write their own key words and since they have found out that these scrawly shapes mean something, they know what they are writing about more than I do.

From here they join in with the stream of autobiographical writing that they all do in the morning output period and a few days of this is enough to show any writer or teacher where style beings. Fives have a most distinctive style. And they write these sentences of the same pattern with its varied content so often that they learn automatically the repeated words and consolidate this style. Without any teaching from me, which transfers the whole question of spelling, word study and composition into the vent of creativity.

This self-chosen vocabulary remains with them, as they rise through the infant room, since in the first place they were part of the mind before they were written at all and in the second place there is this natural repetition. And from them grow a selection of individual vocabularies entered in the back of their writing book where they can be referred to and exchanged. And the standard of spelling which arises from this seems to serve their purpose.

Also there is a general vocabulary springing from their writing which becomes to some modest extent known to most of them sooner or later: then, and, put, went, cowboy, truck, I, inside, outside, pictures, lollies, the, to, on, place, told, me, Daddy, Mummy, because . . .

After a while, as their capacity increases, they write two sentences about themselves and their lives, then three, until six-year-olds are writing half a page and seven-year-olds a page or more a day. But I don't call it teaching: I call it creativity since it all comes from them and nothing from me, and because the spelling and composition are no longer separate subjects to be taught but emerge naturally as another medium.

The drama of these writings could never be captured in a bought book. It could never be achieved in the most faithfully prepared reading books. No one book could ever hold the variety of subject that appears collectively in the infant room each morning. Moreover, it is written in the language that they use themselves. These books they write are the most dramatic and pathetic and colourful things I've ever seen on pages.

But they are private and they are confidences and we don't criticise their content. Whether we read that he hates school or that my house is to be burned down or about the brawl in the pa last night the issue is the same; it is always not what is said but the freedom to say.

I never teach a child something and then get him to write about it. It would be an imposition in the way that it is in art. A child's writing is his own affair and is an exercise in integration which makes for better work. The more it means to him the more value it is to him. And it means everything to him. It is part of him as an arranged subject could never be. It is not a page of sentences written round set words, resulting in a jumble of disconnected facts as you so often see. It is the unbroken line of thought that we cultivate so carefully in our own writing and conversation.

Since writing of this kind is the most exhaustive of all the mediums they use in the output period, I time it early in the morning. Often we break the writing time with expressive dancing since dancing is body-talk anyway. I know for sure that some welcome it and it may help composition, but I don't know.

The whole exercise of creative writing, the reaching back into the mind for something to say, nurtures the organic idea and exercises the inner eye; and it is this calling on the child's own resources that preserves and protracts a little longer his own true personality.

The mechanics of teaching the organic writing

Ten o'clock is back-ache time. By then you have spent an half-hour bending over the children writing at their low desks. But there's no alternative. Not only do you enter the words they ask for at the back of their books, but, bearing in mind the reading of them afterwards, you watch the spacing of the words for better legibility, carefully oversee the grammar and, above all, nurture the continuity of their thought. You correct as they go along, not after.

It's no good sitting at the table and letting the children queue up. That method is self-denounced. You've got to be mobile and available to all. You've got to exercise something like an all-seeing eye all the time and all at once, which makes me think that this period of organic writing drains even more from a teacher than an art period. So that the back-ache of giving equals to the back-ache of bending.

Twelve is the uttermost limit for one teacher. Eight is about the number. I take them when the rest of the room is self-dependant in the development period. The noise doesn't matter. The children writing are just about as talkative as the others. But I let it be like that. Suppression is just the last thing in organic work.

When I had a junior assistant we both got to work. But when I didn't, I would have two senior boys entering the words, a week's worth at a time, while I watch the spacing, the grammar and the line of thought. Maybe some people never knew there was a line of thought in an infant.

But this work soon shows that there is. One of the hazards met in organic writing is the conversation between each other, during which a child tells his neighbour all that he wants to say, so that he skips the necessity of putting it down and writes something like, "Then I went home;" Which closes the subject irrevocably. Against this, however, I don't allow them to write "Then I went home," at all. Giving no reason. So that when they start off, "I went to the pa," the next sequence is what happened at the pa. And once you've got him over that hazard, the line of thought takes care of itself. But it's not a usual risk.

I used to think that a statement of theirs must be finished at all costs at the one sitting; but it turns out that you can close down safely at a definite time, because they can pick up what they were writing the day before with no trouble at all. They just read it over and go on. Although, for all that, the half-hour often extends. It depends on how well or otherwise you are covering the work, which in turn depends on how many you have writing.

With my children there is no occasion to start them off formally. Having been bred on the Key Vocabulary and though the two-word and three-word sentences they start naturally enough. Sometimes I still say, as I did in the K.V., "What are you going to say?" but the need becomes increasingly rare. If, however, one is really stuck, you do what you have done all along; engage him in conversation, and in no time there is the thing off his mind.

Yet there are times when one cannot start. He's just plain not in the mood. You can't always say an important thing because it is the time to say it. Sometimes he will say candidly, "I don't want to write," and that's just what you get him to write: "I don't want to write." From there you ask "Why?" and here comes an account of some grievance or objection which, after all, just as well as any other idea, delivers his mind of what is on it, practises his composition, and wraps him up in what is of interest to himself.

You never want to say that it's good or bad. That's got nothing to do with it. You've got no right at all the criticise the content of another's mind. A child doesn't make his own mind. It's just there. Your job is to see what's in it. Your only allowable comment is one of natural interest in what he is writing. As in conversation. And I never mark their books in any way; never cross out anything beyond helping them to rub out a mistake, never put a tick or a stamp on it and never complain of bad writing. Do we complain of each other's writing in a strongly-felt letter? The attention is on the content. What we feel about his work has got nothing to do with it. The thing is for them to write what is on their minds and if they do or do not accomplish that, it is you who are good or bad. From the teacher's end it boils down to whether or not she is a good conversationalist; whether or not she has the gift or the wisdom to listen to another; the ability to draw out and preserve that other's line of thought. Which refers back to the nature of the teacher. The best juniors I had on this work were the modest, self-effacing kind, while the worst of them was a very clever girl who was an insatiable talker and who in her personal life talked everyone else to pieces on the subject of herself. And in that year I had the lowest level of organic writing on record.

Ten o'clock is back-ache time. But did any fruitful effort ever not bend us? "The labour we long for physics pain."

The Māori Infant Room: No. 4: Organic Reading. *National Education*, 3 April 1956, pp. 97–98

> *"A child comes up, if at all, in accordance with the law of his own growth."*
> —Dr. Burrow

It's a sad thing to say of the vocabulary of any set reading books for an infant room that it must necessarily be a dead vocabulary. Yet I say it. For although the first quality of life is change, these vocabularies never change. Winter and summer, for brown race or white, through loud mood or quiet, the next group of words, related or not to the current temper of the room, inexorably move into place for the day's study.

I tried to meet this division between the climate of a room and an imposed reading book by making another set of books from the immediate material, but all I did was to compose another dead vocabulary. For although they are closer to the Māori children than the books of the upper English middle class, their vocabulary is static too, and it is not the answer to the question I have asked myself for years; What is the organic vocabulary?

At last I know: Primer children write their own books.

First thing every morning this infant room gets under way on organic writing, and it is this writing that I use in relative proportions as the reading for the day; for the children just off the key vocabulary with their stories of two words up to those who can toss off a page or so. In this way we have a set of graded brand new stories each morning, each sprung from the circumstances of their own lives and illustrated unmatchably in the mind.

The new words they have asked for during the morning's writing and which have been entered in the back of their books, they put up on the blackboard each morning. They range in numbers from one or two to ten or so. They reconsider these words after the morning interval when they come in for the intake hour. They read them and spell them for ten minutes. I don't require that they should all be learnt and remembered. If they are important enough they will stay all right, whatever the length. Neither is it for me to sort out which is important. I never say "spell pictures." I say, "Perri, spell one of your words." Then I get the real word and the right spelling. In fact this is a thing that I hand to them. Hearing each other spell. Sometimes, however, we run over these words before dispersing for lunch and what they have picked up from the morning's writing and reading of the organic work, in terms of numbers of new words and their varying difficulties is sometimes a surprise.

Each afternoon, however, all the words, whether known or not, are rubbed from the board and each morning the new ones go up. It's exciting for us all. No one ever knows what's coming. Wonderful words appear: helicopter, lady's place, cowboy, sore ear, fish and chips, dirt, Captain Marble, mumps, superman and King of the Rocket Men. Words following intimately from day to day the classroom mood; echoing the tangi in the district, recounting the pictures in the hall the night before or revealing the drama behind the closed doors of the pa.

This is the main reading of the day. They master their own story first, then tackle someone else's. There is opportunity to read out their own story and it is from this reading that discussions arise. And since every background of every story is well known to all the inner illustration flashes very brightly and the discussions are seldom sluggish.

In reading one another's stories reference is continually made to the writer for the identification of new words. This hardly hurts the writer. Unwittingly, energetically and independently of me, they widen the intake.

How much easier and more pleasant all this is when the stories are followed with a personal interest, and with the whole of the background seen alive in mind. The facts of suitable printing, length of line and intelligibility run nowhere in the race with meaning. As for word recurrence, there occurs a far more natural one here than anything we could work out. A word recurs as long as they want it and is then dropped cold: a word is picked up like a new friend and dropped when he becomes boring. Which is what I mean when I say it is a live vocabulary. Things happen in it.

Since I take this original writing as a basis for reading, a strict watch is kept on grammar and punctuation. And as for the writing itself, the handwriting I mean, it has to be at least the best that they can do, to save their own faces, when changing books. Which brings one more subject into the vent of creativity: handwriting.

This organic reading, however, is not meant to stand alone: it is essentially a lead up and out to all the other reading, and as a child rises through the infant room, reaching further and further out to the inorganic and standard reading, there is a comfortable movement from the inner man outward, from the known to the unknown, from the organic to the inorganic. The thing is to keep it a gracious movement, for it is to the extent that the activity in an infant room is creative that the growth of a mind is good.

The mechanics of teaching organic spelling

After play at eleven during the intake period we turn our attention to the new words themselves. The children pick up their books and run to the blackboard and write them up; the words asked for during the writing of the morning. They're not too long ago to be forgotten. Some of them are, when a child has asked for a lot, but they ask you what they are.

Since they are all on the wall blackboard, I can see them from one position. They write them, revise them, the older children spell them and the younger merely say them, but each child is at his own individual level and working to his own particular capacity. Some of them read the word to me—if the group is too big to get round them all—but they all hear each other. You obtain this necessary "You and me" again. Of course, there is a lot of noise, but there's a lot of work too.

Sometimes I say "Who can spell a word?" and I am given from those who can a word that is instinctively within their compass and which, in any case, is a word of meaning to himself. He wants to spell it. Moreover, attached to this word, is an unaided inner illustration. Spelling evolves easily and cheerfully. True, hard words are abandoned on occasion, according to the relation of the age of the child to the challenge of the word, but often they are industriously learnt owing to their emotional value. Words the size of "sky rocket" get themselves spelt from no drive of mine; "skeleton," "lollies" and so on, while few boys do not know how to spell "cowboy". It's not a hard period for the teacher, this one. Taking in seems to be easier than putting out. Besides [,] the latent energy, the element that so severely opposes a teacher when imposing knowledge, is here turned on what they are doing. It's an energy that is almost frightening when released. True, there is noise to it that some would object to, it being unprofessional; but when did I ever claim to be professional?

The writing up and the spelling of these words take about a quarter of an hour and from here they run with their books to the ring of small chairs prepared beforehand for the reading and exchange of them.

The mechanics of teaching organic reading

About a quarter of an hour for the reading.

You can tell by the state of these books they write daily whether or not the organic reading is going ahead. Contrary to the look of a room, they should end up in tatters. When a teacher handed me a group of books recently in irreproachable condition, I knew that the largest point of the whole organic pattern had been overlooked; the reading of and the discussion of one another's books. All art is communication. We never really make things for ourselves alone. The books are to read to another.

When I had a junior, she took time off to keep abreast of the mending of these books, and when I didn't I made my morning rounds armed with a roll of cello tape as well as a pencil, rubber and razor blade and mended as I went. It was hard at first to pass these dilapidated books to an inspector, but I got over it. Once I had some exercise books made for the purpose at the press, of light drawing paper, with a view to precluding the wear and tear, but although they cost considerably more they tore just the same. The drawing paper should have been of heavier weight. But economy comes into this.

However, I have not yet worked out what would be the easier on the committee funds; the outlay on cello tape or on drawing paper. One young teacher practising the organic work told me she couldn't go on with it until she had mended her books, little realising that from her confession I knew that the work was being thoroughly done.

Sitting in their ring of chairs, the children read again their own and then each other's. I regularly invite them to read aloud to the others. But there's got to be a very light hand or the discussion will not follow. And this discussion is the most significant of all. It is the climax of the whole organic purpose. When we are engaged on this, I arrange that the smaller children are outside for games or story with a junior assistant, or a senior pupil. For the organic writing itself proves to be a startling point of departure into talk that would not occur otherwise. It leads into revelations that range from the entertaining to the outrageous. But, beyond a normal show of interest, you don't comment. You "neither praise nor blame; you observe." You let everything come out, uncensored; otherwise, why do it at all?

About a quarter of an hour for the reading, taking you to half past eleven, then about a quarter of an hour on discussion, on what I call "talk." It may seem a long time for talk in school, but the very least I can say is that I gain knowledge of my material, and the most I can say is that I could never see anything retarding in the "passionate interchange of talk."

The last quarter of the hour from eleven to twelve they read Māori infant readers. It's all intake. I'm not ashamed of eleven till twelve.

The Māori Infant Room: Organic Reading Is Not New. *National Education*, 1 May 1956, p. 141

Organic reading is not new. The Egyptian hieroglyphics were one-word sentences. Helen Keller's first word, "water," was a one-word book. Tolstoy found his way to it in his peasant school, while, out in the field of Unesco today it is used automatically as the only reasonable way of introducing reading to primitive people: in a famine area the teachers wouldn't think of beginning with any words other than "crop, soil, hunger, manure," and the like.

Not that the organic teaching is exclusively necessary to the illiterate of a primitive race. True, it is indispensable in conducting a young child from one culture to another, especially in New Zealand where the Māori is obliged to make the transition at so tender an age, but actually it is universal. First words are different from first drawings only in medium, and first drawings vary from country to country. In New Zealand a boy's first drawing is anything that is mobile; trucks, trains and planes, if he lives in a populated area, and if he doesn't, it's horses. New Zealand girls, however, draw houses first wherever they live. I once made a set of first readers on these two themes. But Tongan children's first drawings are of trees, Samoan five-year-olds draw churches and Chinese draw flowers. What a fascinating story this makes!

How can anyone begin any child on any arranged book, however good the book, when you know this? And how good is any child's book anyway, compared with the ones they write themselves? Of course, as I'm always saying, it's not the only reading: it's no more than the FIRST reading. The bridge.

It's the bridge from the known to the unknown; from a native culture to a new; and, universally speaking, from the inner man out.

Organic reading is not new: first words have ever meant first wants. "Before a nation can be formed," says Voltaire, "it is necessary that some language should be established. They must doubtless have begun by sounds, which must have expressed their first wants … Idioms in the first state must have consists of monosyllables …

"We really find that the most ancient nations who have preserved anything of their primitive tongue, still express by monosyllables the most familiar things which most immediately strike the senses. Chinese to this very hour is founded on monosyllables.

"The Chaldeans for a long time engraved their observations and laws upon bricks in hieroglyphics: these were speaking characters … they therefore, at first, painted what they wanted to communicate. … In time they invented symbolic figures: darts representing war; an eye signified divinity …"

"I told myself," writes Tolstoy of his peasant school, "that in certain cases progress follows an irregular path, and that we have to approach primitive people as naturally as we can, helping them to follow the particular path of progress that they have chosen themselves."

First, he must fathom the mind of the peasant child and let his pupils teach him the art of teaching. In his school his pupils were free to choose their own subjects and to take as much work as they desired, the teacher considering it his duty to adjust his method of approach to the individual child.

These free Tolstoy schools, without forcing the will of a child, were remarkably successful.

International volunteers in Kabylia in the mountains of Algeria:

About twenty children were sitting in front of her under an ash tree and reading in chorus the name of their village which she had written on a big sheet of paper. They were enormously proud; time and time again they read us the word.

But the next evening three of the adults came to ask us to teach them to write their names. "Why do you want to write your name?" One of them explained: "To sign at the Post Office. If I can sign my name to collect a registered letter I shall not need to pay the witnesses."

"And do you often get letters like that?"

"Sometimes. From my son in France."

"We went steadily on; but the evening instead of resting under the mosquito net, we were all caught up in the fever of fundamental education."

Organic reading for beginners is not new: it's our rejection of it that's new.

Nature Study and Number: The Golden Section. *National Education*, 1 August 1956, pp. 248–251

"Many centuries ago Plato and Pythagoras had already found in *number* the clue to the *nature* of the universe and to the mystery of beauty."

But in school it works out to be of more practical importance to realise these two aspects, nature study and number, as differences rather than as the fundamental unity that they are; even though number has never been anything else other than the basis of all forms which nature assumes.

However, the more a subject refers to its source, the more chance it has of being integrated, and although nature study and number are indispensable landmarks in a syllabus, their separation reminds me of the "cutting up of life," to which the Director refers; also I wonder if Tolstoy would have done it this way. I personally see it easier to subordinate them both to a title which has in it the meaning of both. And although there are other deeply-rooted points from which nature study and number arise as a unity there is one which has a particular relation to plant growth: the Golden Section.

The Golden Section is the ideal proportion. It is the division of a distance in such a way that the shorter part is to the longer part as the longer part is to the whole. It's one of the laws governing plant life and although it is something that cannot be explained in an infant room, it can be felt all right and it can be drawn easily and every day. The diminishing spans between twigs on a branch as it tapers to its tip. Or on a fern. Ferns make wonderful counting boards. When we were on long trips when our children were little, we would sometimes give them a big frond to count and as an occupational toy I can recommend it. Costs nothing. Just pick one from the side of the road. And all the time they were learning fundamental things about natural form.

However, to return to the infant room, all this going outside (outside, by the way, has turned out to be a pathetically strong word in the Organic Vocabulary)... all this going outside to see and handle these things and the returning to draw and write about them is the way to find out about this section. The laws of number, nature and beauty turn out to much the same thing.

Yet there is no evidence to suspect the validity of much of the number material available to the infant room; for instance the square things and the many pieces that are built on even numbers; but the idea has its duplicate often enough outdoors. In the right-angled leafing arrangements and the pairs of leaves set exactly opposite each other as in the koromiko. Some of the infant room material has gradations, too; not quite the two-three-five-eight-thirteen combinations of the tapering nodules of plants but gradations anyway. It's an idea to write this sequence on the blackboard for bead-threading purposes, as a variation to the even sets of two, then of three and so on. It's more exciting, seeing the size of the bead-group growing along the string. But the most absorbing number activity is the drawing of a fern frond by the children; ten on this twig, nine on this, eight on this until the one of its own at the end; numbering them.

Then sometimes you can draw a hand in the lower groups, tracing your own hand on the paper and numbering the fingers, when learning to count to five. Or toes. Or a flower with its petals, real flowers outside, unpicked. They make good sums for upper primers, flowers. And it can all happen in a walk and there's nothing destroyed. And there are scents to go with it and beauty.

Clover is an incomparable activity in threes and it's just out the door. Also it is something you can pick in quantities and bring inside. For upper primers learning to count in threes and for the little ones learning to count to three. But counting the impermanent birds is the most concentrated game, involving a self-imposed quiet and watchful eyes and there's the drawing or painting or clay record to follow.

Things don't always work out as ideally as that though. When it's raining or cold we turn to material and chalk. But on a fine morning we all go for a walk down the stop-bank. We count the poplars. We note the fallen leaves. We play games in them and some of the girls dance the Babes in the Wood ballet and cover two children with leaves. We note the turning colour all around and use the word autumn.

We count the children we can see and work out the ones that are missing. The boy who is sent back to school for disobedience makes a subtraction sum and the strays we pick up on our way, the half-past fours, addition. The last time we went we took a small branch each and counted the leaves on them. They ranged from six to seventeen.

Then I told them to count a hundred trees in the willow plantation, touching each tree, and afterwards we went on down to the sand by the river and wrote our numbers with sticks.

The thing about all this is that they like doing it and become easy to teach. But they just as much like the games and weighing and Ludo and snakes and ladders and dominoes and skittles for the winter. And the seven-year-olds try some formal sums, and try to write up to a hundred. There's even a place for how many pennies in a shilling, although maybe that belongs beyond what I call the plastic age of children. At this time when a mind is setting into its permanent future pattern it might just as well set into a pattern akin to nature. There's time enough for formality and respectability afterwards. So we go for long noisy, happy walks along the stop-bank by the river. All sorts of things can happen in a walk, not the least being the experience itself. To write about or talk or draw about. Then the Golden Section becomes inseparable from writing and reading and drawing and conversation. Three ducks on the wing we like better than three ducks on a number card with a static three beside them.

I think that we don't like seeds grown in egg-shells and nasturtiums and onions in tins and a bulb in a jar in the classroom. We like eggs in egg-shells, jam in tins, bulbs in the garden and the nasturtiums by the fence. When we want to see the construction of a seedling there are millions outside. I hate charts as much as they do. I like the moving current of children's interests. Draw the poplars straight after a walk and count them and number them. Then drop the subject for the next. I like the "hot prison of the moment."

We don't waste enough in school. We hoard our old ideas on charts be used again and again like stale bread. Ideas are never the same again, even those of the masters; even if the only change is in our own mood of re-approach. Yet there's never a shortage of ideas if the stimulus is there. Waste the old paper and waste the old pictures and waste the old ideas. It's tidier and simpler.

Birds in our area: Sparrows, mynah, crow, magpie, thrush, blackbird, fantail, fowls, duck, geese.

Unwilling Insects brought into school: Mantis, grasshoppers, caterpillars, snails, beetles, crickets, butterflies.

Uninvited Insects in school: Wasps, lice, bees, spiders.

One early autumn we had the Monarch butterfly caterpillars on the swan plant and watched or tried to watch the sequences of their development into butterflies, but owing to the help given by some of my Māori warriors the butterflies never made it. Over in the junior room, however, they managed to get through.

I think there may be a lack of sympathy between the infant room and the insect world since the enrolment of the wasps. Last week as Arapata was on his way across the playground to get his typhoid injection, a wasp gave him one instead. He got to the nurse all right but not with the same intention. No one pressed him to receive the needle. Not that morning anyway. And when I put Joe outside the other day for discipline's sake, screams told us that the wasps had completed the discipline, so we brought him inside again. We've had no trouble with him since. All of which has provoked passionate discussions on wasps and their ways. Also some passionate paintings.

The birds have supplied us with movements for expressive dancing. There's a magpie dance and a lark dance, although we have seen no larks. We've been told that there are larks, however, but not the spectacular high-flying, high-singing ones. The falling leaves supply us with endless dance design, both formal and informal, also the fin-movement of fish. And frogs. We've had some frogs inside in tins of muddy grassy water for observation but once more the loving ways of my warriors bring their lives to an early close. Also the frogs of these parts are great jumpers and for some reason prefer the machine drawer or the coal tin to the cool water. And get themselves mixed up in the clay bucket or go for the books.

Sammy Snail is the only visitor who has the sense to keep out of reach, dangling on the rafter. And a chrysalis or two. Pussy doesn't get much of a time when she strolls in and I don't think the ginger-rooster will ever call again.

Informal Visitors to the infant room: Sammy Snail, Ginger Rooster, pussy, Mangu's dog, a fantail, a monkey.

We had some goldfish to watch for a time. They were kept in the senior room and were a great draw to the infants. But owing to the container leaking they were put in the tub in the laundry to ensure the automatic replacement of water but one laundry day some soap fell in. . . . Amen.

I have gathered over the years a collection of pictures, however, of different topics, some of them animals, some of them birds, along with the nursery rhymes and seasonal pictures, and mounted them and I keep them in separate packets. Wet day stuff. And they greatly widen the horizon. There's a packet of about thirty pictures of bears, for instance, to follow up on the Three Bears story. Autumn pictures, horse pictures, bird pictures and cat pictures. But they are used for the observation of nature only when we are short of the real live thing; kicking, crawling, singing or stinging.

I place the Golden Section in the Output period between one o'clock and two. Either for the whole of the time, as during a walk, or a number lesson outside to be written about when they come in, or for part of the time. So much depends on mood and weather and attendance. The pictures, though, occur in the Intake period between eleven and twelve.

The formal number scheme which is provided for our use is essentially creative and belongs in the morning.

Also one soon collects seasonal songs and poems and stories about animals and birds and weather, e.g.:

SPRING

Songs: Buttercups and Daisies; Hark, Hark, the Lark; the North Wind.

Poems: Chick-chick; Violet; Jonquil.

Stories: The Black Cat; The Apple-blossom.

SUMMER

Songs: The Birds in the Trees; Catching Fishes.

Poems: Kees-kees; Lady-bird.

Stories: Miscellaneous; Little Red Hen.

AUTUMN

Songs: The Falling Leaves; Rustle, Rustle; A Little Brown Baby.

Poem: Ten Little Yellow Leaves.

Stories: Miscellaneous; Janet and John stories.

WINTER

Songs: The South Wind; Jolly Little Eskimo; Mr. Wind; Pitter-patter; The Rain Fairy.

Poems: Children, Children; Jack Frost.

Story: The Three Goats.

Flowers in our area: Marigolds, stock, roses, poppies, currant, pansies, geranium, dahlia, delphinium.

Trees in our area: Cabbage trees, macrocarpa, hoheria, walnut, most fruit trees, pine.

Experience and record could well be the story of the Golden Section. There can't be any tight compartments of age or time or work coverage. I think that this relation of number and nature study to their deep common source may give back in integration what it takes from the expertly-planned lesson. At least as much. And I think that if we take care of the Golden Section, its parts, nature study and number will, in the infant room anyway, take care of themselves.

Organic Teaching: The Unlived Life. *National Education*, 3 September 1956, pp. 294–295

It's all so merciful on a teacher, this appearance of the subjects of an infant room in the creative vent. For one thing the drive is no longer the teacher's but the children's own. And for another the teacher is at last with the stream and not against it; the stream of children's inexorable creativeness. As Dr. Jung says, psychic life is world power that exceeds by many times all the powers of the earth; as Dr. Burrow says, the secret of our collective ills is to be traced to the suppression of creative ability; and as Erich Fromm says, destructiveness is the outcome of the unlived life.

So it is more than professional moment that all of the work of young children should be through the creative vent. It is more than a teaching matter or a dominion one. It's an international matter. So often I have said in the past, when the war is over the statesman should not go into conference with one another but should turn their attention to the infant rooms since it is from there that comes peace or war. And that's how I see the organic teaching. It helps to set the creative pattern in a mind while it is yet malleable and in this role is a humble contribution to peace.

The expansion of a child's mind can be a beautiful growth. And in beauty are included the qualities of equilibrium, harmony and rest. There's no more comely word in the language than "rest." All the movement in life and out of it too, is towards a condition of rest. Even the simple movement of a child "coming up."

I can't disassociate the activity in an infant room from peace and war. So often I have seen the destructive vent, beneath an onslaught of creativity, dry up under my eyes. Especially with the warlike Māori five-year-olds who pass through my hands in hundreds, arriving with no other thought in their heads other than to take, break, fight and be first. With no opportunity for creativity they may well develop as they did in the past with fighting as their ideal of life. Yet all this can be expelled through the creative vent and the more violent the boy the more I see that he creates, and when he kicks the others with his big boots, treads on fingers on the mat, hits another over the head with a piece of wood or throws a stone, I put clay in his hands or chalk. He can create bombs if he likes or draw my house in flames but it is the creative vent that is widening all the time and the destructive one atrophying, however much it may look to the contrary. And anyway I have always been more afraid of the weapon unspoken than of the one on the blackboard.

With all this in mind therefore I try to bring as many facets of teaching into the creative vent as possible with emphasis on reading and writing. And that's just what organic teaching is; all subjects in the creative vent. It's just as easy for a teacher, who can give a child a brush and let him paint to give him a pencil and let him write, and to let him pass his story to the next one to read. Simplicity is too safe. There's no occasion whatever for the early imposition of a dead reading, a dead vocabulary. I'm so afraid of it. It's like a frame over a young tree making it grow in an unnatural shape. It makes me think of that curtailment of a child's expansion of which Erich Fromm speaks, of that unlived life of which destructiveness is the outcome. "And instead of the wholeness of the expansive tree we have only the twisted and stunted bush." The trouble is that a child from a modern respectable home suffers such a serious frame on his behaviour long before he comes near a teacher. Nevertheless I think that after a year of organic work the static vocabularies can be used without misfortune. It can even, under the heads of external stimulus and respect for the standard of English, become desirable.

But only when built upon the organic foundation. And there's hardly anything new in the conception of progress from the known to the unknown. It's just that when the inorganic reading is imposed first it interferes with integration and it's upon the integrated personality that everything is built. We've lost the gracious movement from the inside outward. We overlook the footing. I talk sometimes about a bridge from the pa to the European environment but there is a common bridge for a child of any race and of more moment than any other which is the bridge from the inner world outward. And that is what the organic teaching is. An indispensable step in integration. Without it we get this one-patterned mind of the New Zealand child, accruing from so much American influence of the mass-mind type. I think that we already have so much pressure towards sameness, through radio, film and comic outside the school that we can't afford to do a thing inside that is not toward individual development and from this stance I can't see that we can indulge in the one imposed reading for all until the particular variety of a mind is set. And a cross-section of children from different places in New Zealand (I own 70 fancy dress costumes which I lend) provides me with an automatic check on the progress of the one-patterned mind. All the children want the same costumes. If you made dozens of cowboy and cowgirl costumes, hundreds of supermen and thousands of rocket men costumes and hired them at half-a-guinea a go, you'd get every penny of it and would make a fortune vast enough to retire on and spend the rest of your life in the garden. As for my classics, Bo-Peep, the Chinese Mandarin, Peter Pan and the Witch and so on so gather the dust that they have had to be folded and put away. It's this sameness in children that can be so boring. So is death boring.

To write peaceful reading books and put them in an infant room is not the way to peace. They don't even scratch the surface. No child ever asked for a Janet or a John costume. There is only one answer to destructiveness and that is creativity. And it never was and never will be any different. And when I say so I am in august company.

I like unpredictability and variation; I like drama and I like gaiety; I like peace in the world and I like interesting people and all this means that I like life in its organic shape and that's just what you get in an infant room where the creative vent widens. For this is where style is born in both writing and art, for art is the way you do a thing and an education based on art at once flashes out style. The word "jalopy" made its fascinating appearance the other day. Brian wrote "I went to town. I came back on a jalopy bus." This word stirred us. The others cross-questioned him on the character of such a bus. It turned out to mean "rackety" and although the word was picked up at once nevertheless they still ask for it to go up on the spelling list. We haven't had jalopy for spelling lately, Brian says. He loves spelling it, which is what I mean when I say that the drive is the children's own. It's all so merciful on a teacher.

Inescapably war and peace wait in an infant room; wait and vie.

True the toy shops are full of guns, boys' hands hold tanks and war planes while the blackboards, clay boards and easels burst with warplay. But I'm unalarmed. My concern is the rearing of the creative disposition, for creativity in this crèche of living where people can still be changed must in the end defy, if not defeat the capacity for destruction. Every happening in the infant room is either creative or destructive; every drawing, every shaping, every sentence and every dance goes one way or the other. For "life has an inner dynamism of its own; it tends to grow, to be expressed, to be lived. The amount of destructiveness in a child is proportionate to the amount to which the expansiveness of his life has been curtailed. Destructiveness is the outcome of the unlived life."

I believe in this as passionately as the artist in his brush and the roadman in his shovel. For every work, and first of all that of a teacher, must have its form, its design. And the design of my work is that creativity in this time of life when character can be influenced for ever is the solution to the problem of war. To me it has the validity of a law of physics and all the unstatable, irrepressible emotion of beauty.

TONE ("The still centre"—T. S. Eliot). *National Education,* 1 October 1956, pp. 342–343

Tone belongs to order and can be won.

It concerns not only classrooms; it is a condition that is or is not implicit in every group of people working together over something, from infant rooms through education departments to groups as big as countries. For in the running of all these, order is the key. It's the expression on the countenance of a group.

But there are two kinds of order and which is the one we wish for: Is it the conscious order that ends up as respectability? Or is it the unconscious order that looks like chaos on the top? There is a separate world on each side of this question mark.

When we track tone to its source we find that it inhabits the temperament area. We find that the person with tone is not badly disturbed by passions. Following it further beyond temperament it turns out to be, to a large extent, a particular climate of the soul. As the Czech architect, Honzig, says in speaking of the final form of a building, "It is a condition of rest."

However, whichever kind of order teachers think about, tone is still qualified by the same three things: the personality of the teacher, the personality of the children and the method used.

I know a teacher who takes tone with her wherever she goes; whether to the infant department of a big school, to an outsized choir in the municipal or to a Red Cross demonstration in a shop window. Whether you meet her in a drawing room, in an infant room, in the street or backstage, you meet tone too. Also I know a headmaster who doesn't have to try to bring a feeling of peace upon the standards and I've had two out of six juniors who, although they know nothing of the conscious cultivation of tone, nevertheless carried it about in their pockets. But none of these people is discomforted with the "restless passions that would not be stilled." And they have tone; inside and out.

Happily, however, the structure of a teacher is not the whole of the formula for tone in a classroom. There's the tone of the children and the tone of the district. On the east coast, where our neighbours were Sir Apirana Ngata on one side and Reweti Kohere on the other, no upheaval in the school could shake its tone. Whatever the incident, and we were not without it, the tone remained unscratched. The district itself had tone. The people had sitting among them authentic leaders and all remained well. There was serenity. It flowed down from "The Sir" through the Ngatiporou like the influence of a headmaster through his school.

But here, where there never has been a leader and where the Māoris walk precariously the tightrope between the brown and the white, there is none of the tribal confidence and cohesion of the coast. So there's no order or calm in the district and if a teacher can't supply the missing quality from his own resources or by his own method the days can turn into outlawry.

But not necessarily, for tone can be won. Even when it is missing in the teacher and missing in the children. There's method left. The thing is to forget about appearances and cultivate the order in the unconscious. Which is simple enough and done with creativity. And although the room will seem disorderly by sight, it is not so by feel. Through the vents of creativity forces can get out and away, leaving the lower levels relatively calm. There's a noisy kind of peace through the long creative periods in the morning when every child is engrossed in some medium of construction. True, this infant room is fed by a loud-mouthed and disintegrated pa, but I don't feel hopeless. You can put every subject into the creative vent so that there can be a flow and a release of forces all day. The noise is terrible, but you've got to pay in some way. I sort out the unseemly habits and train seemly ones. I rehearse the periods in mind before we have them. I try to get reciprocal respect and trust between me and them. I go to any lengths in the pursuit of style in their work and continually check up on the feel of the room. All of which another teacher possessing natural tone doesn't need to do. But in spite of the unrest in the tribe and the lack of cohesion in the pa and the "fire that on my bosom preys," I get a precarious sense of some deep order.

And then, when you come to think about it, you find that of the two kinds of order, the conscious and the unconscious orders, only one is real. It's the order in the deep hidden places. And whatever the temperament of the teacher and of the children, it is accessible to anyone. When we trace tone beyond the area of temperament and beyond the climate of the personality to its origin, we find that it is simply this order. The true order in the depths. The "still centre."

Workbook

Teachers say they need their workbooks.

They say, I can't rely on myself in the melee of a lesson to work out sequences on the spot. When the time comes I need everything at my fingertips. I've got to have it all thought out beforehand.

Conception in tranquillity can range from the conscious condensation of material and method up to the level of prayer. All the great teachers of the past have drawn their action from non-action. From Christ upon the high mountain, through Lo Tung over his tea down to us. And I can never see that these names are too big to be used side by side with today. The intention is the same—teaching. It's not this conception in tranquillity that is the point of departure.

I know that the preparation of a workbook may clarify to a teacher what he is thinking about. I know that the order and method of it reflect inescapably upon the minds of the children. And I suspect from what I see that the very fact of a workbook evokes on the mind of a teacher in reliable peace. And that its notes mean that necessary stepping stone between his conception and his execution. Indeed, I can believe comfortably enough that the assessment of a workbook can be truthfully close to the assessment of a man. It is neither the fact of a workbook nor its phase in teaching that is the point of departure. It's the incorrigible variety in man himself.

For some teachers just don't see a workbook in this way. True, they see it in the same place between conception and execution, but not as a stepping stone. To some teachers the workbooks is the middleman intercepting some of the energy and glamour directed upon the canvas. Leonardo da Vinci cut straight into his marble, Rabindranath Tagore wrote his verses neat and I didn't hear of Jesus making notes. Teachers, all of them, in one medium or another, who mistrusted the middleman.

To the extent that a teacher is an artist, and according to Plato there should be no distinction, his inner eye has the native power, unatrophied, to hold the work he means to do. And in the places where he can't see, he has a trust in himself, that he will see it, either in time for the occasion or eventually. And he would rather risk a blank in his teaching than expend cash on the middleman. He wants the feel of the glamour of direct engagement. He wants to see in his mind, as he teaches, the idea itself, rather than the page it is written on. He wants to work from conception itself directly upon the children without interference from the image of its record on a book. He wants to work in a way that to him is clear, without conflict and without interception.

It doesn't always, I think, clarify a teacher's thoughts to note them down. To some it is a pinioning. Something to evade. I learnt when I was a very small girl that you could leave half your meaning behind in a preparatory sketch. When I was very young I worked straight from my mind upon the clay. Then I knew that what I did was all of what I could do and not just the residue of a trial. And when in teaching I found that I was required to precede all my work with the written notes of a workbook, it was with gross payment to the middleman that I did so.

In an infant room, however, where the activity is wholly expressive, with all subjects allowed their legitimate entry into the area of creativity, the question of a workbook can hardly arise. Wherever there's creativity on a large scale, there's life and I anyway, can't plot life. I just join in. How are we to know what is going to come from the children on this day or that? How can I tell what the reading and spelling is going to be since each morning they write their own books for the day's use? Does a teacher wish to anticipate the purposes of each new day? In an infant room cultivating the organic expansion, a teacher learns to put the factors of mood and change before the prognostications of a workbook.

As Caldwell Cook says: Not the professor, but the artist, is your true school master.

Dancing

Dancing I place in the morning output time, considering it as good a medium as any other, since Plato said it was the one complete expression involving the faculties on all levels, spiritual, intellectual and physical. That's what I think too. Not that I deliberately teach it for that reason. It just happened one bright spring morning when I was playing some Schubert to please no one but myself that a child stood up from its work and began composing a dance, then another, then another, and there it all was. And here it all still is.

Although most of the interpretations come from them, I indulge myself by providing them with a further selection of movements to use as they choose, to supplement their own movements. But I haven't noticed much of it being used voluntarily in their interpretation of new music. The old story of imposition again.

I never use other than classical music. Not only for my own sake but because it was a classic that brought them to their feet in the first place. So far I have used Schubert, Beethoven, Tchaikovsky, Chopin, Brahms and Grieg. But I'm only feeling my way since my only source of dancing knowledge is from my own dreaming.

My aim is that a child may be able to create dancing as freely as he draws or writes autobiography or plays. But I haven't got there yet. Although we place dancing in the output period, also we use it to break any strain of work during the day.

References

Hood, L. (1988). *Sylvia! The biography of Sylvia Ashton-Warner.* Auckland: Viking.

CHAPTER 3

Sylvia's place: Ashton-Warner as New Zealand educational theorist

Sue Middleton

Sylvia Ashton-Warner's New Zealand educational context has been—and continues to be—misrepresented as antithetical to her creative methods. Sue Middleton, a professor of education, locates Sylvia's educational ideas within the national and international Progressive Education movement, indicating that key education officials in postwar New Zealand encouraged creativity and self-expression.

Sylvia Ashton-Warner frequently claimed her educational ideas to be "in confrontation ... with the time and place in which she lived" (Clemens, 1996, p. 23). But, as one North American educational philosopher has put it, "an educational theory grows where it is planted, soaking up the nutrients in the local soil, turning to the local light" (Grumet, 1988, p. 14).

This chapter makes the case that, as a teacher, an educational writer and theorist, Sylvia Ashton-Warner grew in, and not in spite of, New Zealand. My argument unfolds in two parts. The first reviews theoretical ideas in the local and international educational environment in which Sylvia lived and worked. Sylvia and Keith Henderson taught in what was referred to until 1947 as the Native School system (and from 1948 until its abolition in 1968 as the Maori School system).[1] They trained and began work as teachers during the Depression; and Sylvia began serious writing during World War Two. The war and the Native School system intersected in complex ways with the wider international Progressive Education movement and its promotion "from the top" in New Zealand's public schools. An overview of Progressive (or New) Education, the changing theories of culture and race in the Native School system, and relations between these during World War Two, opens a wide-angled aperture through which to read Sylvia's early writing.

The second part of the chapter zooms in on the schoolrooms, hills and sheds in which Sylvia Ashton-Warner read, thought and wrote, particularly during the World War Two years when the family lived in Pipiriki. At this time, Sylvia learned the disciplined life of a writer, keeping a diary in which she developed her educational theory. This would later be published as *Myself* (1967b). I trace footprints of others who engaged with Sylvia in these spaces, finding pathways

---

[1] For a history of New Zealand's Native School system, see Barrington (2008); Barrington & Beaglehole (1974); Simon (1998); Simon & Tuhiwai Smith (2001).

that connect the reading-writing-thinking Sylvia on her bush-clad hilltops and inside her haunted shacks with wider metropolitan networks of educational thought.

Sylvia's list: Educational theory in New Zealand

Educational theories are expressed in a range of printed texts: academic, political, professional and popular. As a formal body of knowledge, Education is a subject, or discipline, taught and examined in universities. In Sylvia's New Zealand, scope for academic expression in Education was minimal: in 1950, there were only 17 university staff in Education spread across four university colleges and there were no academic Education journals.[2] Educational theories flow between academic and wider public domains, infusing research reports, curriculum documents, teachers' magazines, conference presentations, parliamentary debates and popular media. Politically mandated educational theories colour the gaze of authorities (such as inspectors of schools). As performative scripts (syllabi, programmes and textbooks), educational theories are enacted in everyday classroom settings, giving shape to teachers' work and underpinning the rules, maxims, guidelines, habits and hunches in teaching practice. The spatial arrangements of classrooms, the equipment and the activities in them, are "stagings" of theories of teaching and learning. What children are asked to do and how they are disciplined are performances, or enactments, of theory. Educational theories produce particular kinds of learner and teacher identities.

From the time of Empire, the educational theories of the English-speaking world were global phenomena reaching New Zealand, with metropolitan England as their originating and legitimating authority. Historian Peter Gibbons suggests that we New Zealanders

---

2   My analysis of "Sylvia's place" in Education as an academic subject in New Zealand is developed in another paper (Middleton, 2006).

conceptualise "the seas about these islands" not as barriers but as "highways" (2003, p. 6). What overseas and local conceptual resources were available to Sylvia Ashton-Warner to "think with" and how might these have reached the rooms in which she read and wrote at Pipiriki? Sylvia left us with lists of her reading, including

> Rousseau, Herbert Read, comparative religions, the Bible, Gerard Manley Hopkins, Blake and Coleridge; the English poets, French literature, history and poetry; Russell, Freud, Jung, Adler, and Fromm: Maori mythology, history, culture and the language; the lives of the musicians, music textbooks, and even ploughed through Havelock Ellis, believe it or not. Everything but education. (*I Passed This Way*, 1979/1980, p. 354)

This list links Sylvia Ashton-Warner's reading and writing with the global production and circulation of texts and ideas of her time. By what routes did books by European intellectuals reach the isolated hills of Pipiriki? Some of the systems through which Sylvia encountered her books were initiatives of New Zealand's first Labour government (1937–49): teachers' correspondence courses, book clubs and the Country Library Service[3] (this service was supported by America's Carnegie Corporation).

The books she identifies here are significant. Although Sylvia claimed not to read Education, her list included foundational theories of the international Progressive (or New) Education movement: developmental psychology (Ellis), sociology/social philosophy (Fromm, Rousseau) and psychoanalysis (Freud, Jung and Adler). In *Teacher*, she acknowledged three progressive educational theorists. Two were of the psychoanalytic tradition: Herbert Read[4] and (in a brief aside) A. S. Neill's *Summerhill* (1968). In *Teacher* (1963, p. 90),

---

3   These are referred to in *Myself* (Ashton-Warner, 1967b).
4   Herbert Read's *Education Through Art* (1958) is mentioned in several of Sylvia's texts. He wrote the foreword to *Teacher* and visited Sylvia in New Zealand; for details, see Hood (1988).

she quoted Caldwell Cook: "Not the professor, but the artist, is your true school master".[5] Caldwell Cook's *The Play Way* (1917) (alongside works by Dewey and other progressives) was recommended reading in the 1929 official curriculum that was in place when Sylvia started teaching ("Reports of the Minister of Education", 1928–1956).[6]

Officialdom's engagements with progressive ideas in the years leading up to, during, and after World War Two can be traced in the reports of Ministers of Education ("Reports of the Minister of Education", 1928–1956), Chief Inspectors of Primary Schools ("Reports of the Chief Inspectors of Primary Schools", 1928–1956) and Chief Inspectors of Native Schools ("Reports of the Chief Inspectors of Native Schools", 1928–1956). These show that along the ocean highways, ships carried teachers on exchange visits, delegates to international conferences, books on educational theory, professional journals and curriculum resources. Despite, and to some extent because of, the Great Depression and the war, the 1930s and 1940s were a time of great excitement, experimentation and unprecedented freedom in many educational circles in New Zealand. New "child-centred" methods would foster healthy and happy individual child development, nurture and protect fragile democratic values, and (following Dewey) help build a more democratic society.[7]

Founded during World War One, the international New Education Fellowship (NEF) and its journal *New Era* had members and readers in New Zealand from the 1920s (Abbiss, 1998). In 1937 (when Keith

---

5 See also Ashton-Warner's 1956 article "Tone", reprinted in Chapter 2, this volume.

6 The progressive strands of the 1929 curriculum and Sylvia's reference to Caldwell Cook in *Teacher* are outlined in Middleton (2006).

7 As described elsewhere (May, 2003; Middleton & May, 1997), American philosopher John Dewey had a major impact on many New Zealand early childhood and infant teachers between the 1920s and 1950s. Middleton (2006) indicated that the lengthy reading list in the 1928 "Red Book" curriculum (Department of Education, 1929) included several books by Dewey, including his *Democracy and Education* (1916).

was starting teaching and Sylvia was a wife and young mother in rural Taranaki) the NEF held a conference in four New Zealand centres with support from the new Labour government. Schools were closed to enable teachers to attend and nearly 6,000 of them took the opportunity. Parents, officials and members of the general public showed keen interest. Many were turned away when halls were filled to capacity. A number of the lectures by the 14 international speakers were broadcast nationally on radio, and 2,500 of the 3,000 advance copies of the proceedings presold (Campbell, 1938). As Helen May (2003) outlines, British child psychoanalyst and infant educator Susan Isaacs was particularly popular. The following statement from one of Isaacs' talks encapsulates New Education

> The principle of activity expresses the empirically discovered truth that the child grows by his own efforts and his own real experiences. Whether it be in skill or knowledge, in social feeling or spiritual awareness, it is not what we do to the child or for the child that educates him, but what we enable him to do for himself. (1938, p. 83)

From the 1930s, the language of Progressive (New) Education dominated the writing of education officials, ministers, politicians and inspectors, and surfaced in inservice courses and curriculum resources. In his final report as Chief Inspector of Primary Schools in 1952, Mr F. C. Lopdell reflected

> Until after the First World War, the search was for more suitable subject-matter and better techniques for teaching it, but in the "twenties", largely as a result of the War, education began to set itself the wider objective of developing the whole person for life in a democracy, and the search began for achieving that objective. (p. 2)

He saw the "shift from teaching to learning" as having social objectives

> 'the fuller development of each person is the school's contribution to one of the problems of democracy—the problem of producing a population of independent and socially responsible citizens.' (p. 2)

The "activity" approach to learning in New Education became particularly influential in Native School policy, especially after 1930s, when Douglas Ball was appointed as their Chief Inspector

> [An] essential of social and individual well-being is re-creation, the strengthening of personality, which involves the whole man and is rooted in the unity of life. Beyond physical health, development of mind and character, appreciation of Nature and of art, re-creation is that from which flows the inspirational force that gives life its meaning. The Maori, once strong in racial idealism, is in need of this integration of character. The means adopted to assist in this strengthening of personality is the method of child activity, the encouragement of growth through exercise of emotional and intellectual powers, other than the mere acquisition of knowledge by absorption. (Ball, 1936, p. 2)

Native Schools would provide "a kind of education which shall be closely related to Māori life and culture, and yet shall at the same time form a basis for the social and economic fusion of the two races" (Mason, 1940). This replaced the earlier policy of assimilation, described as follows

> When I first visited Maori schools in 1931 I was impressed by the fact that there was practically nothing Maori in the schools except the Maori children. No Maori song was ever sung, there was no sign of Maori crafts, nor any interest in Maori history as part of the school curriculum. The values in their own culture were ignored, and the instruction was on Pakeha lines. (Fletcher, 1948, p. 2)

In 1931, a book of conference proceedings, *Maori and Education*, was "the first work in the Principles of Education, Pakeha or Maori, that has yet appeared in New Zealand" (Jackson, 1931, xiii). At the turn of the 20th century, Māori had been presumed a dying race, and Education Professor A. G. Fitt of Auckland University College saw schooling as sharing responsibility for this: "We do not educate the Maori but rather we unwittingly assist in killing him in the spiritual sense of the word. And, with this spiritual killing, the physical death is not far off" (1931, p. 223). He debated the question of fusion

> To return to the Maori, we must consider for a moment the problem as to whether his ultimate end (if indeed he survive long enough) will be fusion with the white race or the maintenance of a separate existence alongside his countrymen. If the former case holds, and many high authorities on the Maori consider it will, then the education of the Maori must frankly face the problem of fusion. If the latter holds, it must be subject to certain limits, for much of the Maori's earlier life is quite inconsistent with our white civilisation. In fact, in this case too, it will not be the original culture which will survive, but a culture considerably modified in the direction of our white culture. (p. 225)

While this and other chapters of *Maori and Education* bear imprints of previous assimilationist language, the book was a scholarly application of the anthropological, psychological and pedagogical concepts of its time to educational questions, including bilingualism, Māori "mentality" and Māori "educability". It was "essential for administrators and teachers concerned with Native education to study and understand the culture of the people in whose interests they are employed" (Ball, 1936, p. 7). Sylvia's list of her readings included "Maori mythology, history, culture and the language".

As in the chapters by Penfold and Tawhiwhirangi in this book, the objective of "fusion" did not extend to the use of Māori language as a medium of instruction, bilingualism being seen as an obstacle to "progress". However, teachers were encouraged to create supplementary reading materials, consistent with the children's vocabularies, as stated in the report of the Chief Inspector of Maori Schools in 1948

> Even in the infant room, in such a subject as reading, there is too much reliance on textbooks, to the neglect of the most effective material—the teacher's own blackboard and self-prepared reading matter. It must be admitted that the primer readers as supplied to the schools, have

serious deficiencies, but so far there is nothing better available to supplant them as textbooks. They are not written for Maori children, and contain words that are unnecessary for a Maori child's vocabulary. The need is all the greater, therefore, to supplement these books by suitable reading material. A study of the words needed by the Maori child should be one of the first points to be considered. (Fletcher, 1948, p. 2)

These comments echo the 1929 curriculum, which had urged teachers to feel free to adapt their programmes to "the interests of the pupils and to the environment in which they live" (Atmore, 1929, p. 2)

Both the department's and Sylvia's methods were designed to tap into the Māori child's everyday vocabulary. The department's rationale was sociological: children's words were referential, emanating from their "outside" environments of family, farm and countryside. In contrast, Ashton-Warner looked "inside", "drawing key words out" of each little reader's psychic underworld. It had been her psychotherapist who had taught Sylvia about the two great instincts, fear and sex, during her "nervous breakdown", and her therapeutic insights infused Sylvia's teaching. Sylvia's reading of psychoanalytic literature (Freud, Adler, Jung and others) brought therapy and teaching together in theoretical, as well as experiential, terms. In Sylvia's infant room, children's key words erupted to the surface as captions for the two great drives, fear and sex. The most powerful words were *ghost* and *kiss*: "Any child, brown or white, on the first day remembers those two words from One-Look" (Sylvia, 1956b, p. 11). In the 1950s, Sylvia published the first version of her teaching scheme (which would later become *Teacher*) in serialised form, in *National Education*, the magazine of the NZEI (as reprinted in this volume, Chapter 2). Published under the name "Sylvia", these were her first textual footprints across local landscapes of educational theory.

The official education policies of fusion (or cultural integration) were designed to restore "pride of race". In particular, Native Schools were to cultivate "an interest in the old Maori arts and crafts, in their songs and dances, in their games, and in their history and mythology" (Fletcher, 1948, p. 2). In his 1936 report, Senior Inspector Ball reported on a series of inservice courses for Native School teachers on modern methods of teaching at which Sir Apirana Ngata, Dr Wi Repa and "a large staff of assistants" gave "practical instruction in Maori carving, flax plaiting, tukutuku and taniko work, and poi dancing" (p. 3). Ball's ideas on the educational value of creative and performing arts drew on, and intertwined with, his interests in Māori culture and in New Education. Consistent with this combination, Sylvia's list included poetry, music, Māori history, language and culture. Ball argued that in Native Schools "art and craft may prove to be one of the most productive channels for the growth of individuality and for the development of self-reliance and independence" (1939, p. 3). In *Teacher*, Sylvia wrote, "The Maori mind is essentially artistic in character" (1963, p. 138). Ball said, "The Maori child has a real facility for drawing action pictures of men, horses, aeroplanes and motor vehicles" (1939, p. 3). The boys in Sylvia's infant classes included these words in their key vocabularies. In Ball's scheme, as in New Education more generally, poetry was accorded an important place. He noted in 1939

> Both children and audience reflect the intense pleasure derived from a vivacious and sympathetic interpretation of poetry. When this spirit of brightness has been attained it permeates the whole curriculum, for the children, conscious of their ability to express themselves forcefully, and inspired with self-confidence, are able to convert all their work into pleasure, and the school becomes a hive of industry, with the pupils taking a very active part in their own instruction. (p. 3)

But while concepts of progressivism and cultural integration threaded through educational documents, we know that mandated theories are not always put into practice: they can be resisted, subverted, distorted or ignored. The shifts in thinking were occurring during wartime, when families, teachers, schools and bureaucracies experienced rationing, shortages and the requisition of facilities for military purposes. The high proportion of male teachers in the forces (in 1944 it was 70 percent) (Overton, 1945, p. 1), necessitated the return to the classroom of elderly teachers accustomed to older, authoritarian methods. Family life was disrupted, and children traumatised, by wartime terrors, losses and death. Clarence Beeby, Director-General of Education, advised teachers to apply the principles of developmental psychology to "act as a buffer between the world of the child and the warring world of the adult, to pass on to the child only such of the jarrings and jostlings of the adult world as he feels the childish mind can cope with at this stage. It is for the skilled teacher to say what burden of knowledge the child at each age can bear" (Beeby, 1992, p. 129).

Wartime conditions also encouraged classroom improvisation and experiment. The Department of Education organised conferences of advisors for infant methods promoting activity methods in schools, reporting: "The latest methods of infant room teaching were stimulated by the visits of the infant-teaching specialists to our schools" (Stubbs, 1943, p. 1). The absence of men threw the customary gender order into disarray. Although the wives of the headmaster had usually been expected to teach primer classes in small Māori schools, during the war years, and also during the teacher shortages of the postwar baby boom, any prejudice against married women continuing to teach in public schools subsided, and teaching was seen as women's patriotic duty. Wartime conditions saw even young women rapidly promoted (albeit temporarily) into senior positions as principals, advisers, inspectors and officials. The department reported that some of "these ladies have conducted refresher courses for native school infant teachers" (Stubbs, 1942,

p. 3). Sylvia attended at least one of these courses (see Hood, 1988, p. 105). Throughout the 1930s and 1940s, examples of progressive and experimental teaching were recorded in official reports, and later in Barrington's (1987) study of Native School teachers' logbooks, in interview-based studies of teaching practice in public schools in general (Middleton & May, 1997) and in Native Schools in particular (Simon, 1998; Simon & Tuhiwai Smith, 2001).

Sylvia's books make occasional reference to progressive tendencies in her wider New Zealand educational landscape. Local educators supportive of her approach are seldom referred to by name; more often their identities were disguised. Hood's research has since unmasked some of these hidden identities. Notable New Zealand educators who "passed her way" included: Sir Apirana Ngata (Māori MP, intellectual and educator);[8] Gordon Tovey (National Advisor for Art and Craft, who introduced her to Herbert Read's work);[9] Gwen Somerset (pioneer Progressive infant teacher);[10] Walter Harris (Advisor on Visual Aids);[11] Rowland Lewis (an inspector sympathetic to New Education); and Douglas Ball (Senior Inspector of Native Schools, and later of primary schools).[12] Beeby is cited by name as

---

8 Ashton-Warner mentions Apirana Ngata in *Teacher* (1963, p. 85). She also mentions Ngata in *Greenstone*: Koro (her character Huia's great-grandfather) was a teacher at Te Aute College "where he had a hand in schooling young Maoris designed for Pacific renown later in the century: Ngata, Pomare and Rangi Hiroa, with ripples of letters after their name and European titles" (1967a, p. 51).
9 For further information about Tovey's work, see Simpson (1974).
10 Gwen Somerset (née Alley) is well known as a pioneer of Progressive methods in infant classrooms. In *Myself* (1967b, p. 101), Sylvia refers to a visit and letter from "Saul's brother, a big name in the education world". Saul was the alias Sylvia used for her close friend, the district nurse Joy Alley. Hood (1988, p. 102) refers to Joy having a visit from her sister Gwen in Pipiriki. Gwen's methods, as described in her autobiography (1988), were similar to Sylvia's. See also McDonald, this volume.
11 The idea that the character of Pan is based on Walter Harris is discussed in Hood (1988).
12 For a discussion of Sylvia Ashton-Warner's depiction of Douglas Ball, see Middleton (2006).

an advocate of holistic or integrated curriculum in *Teacher* (and also in the serialised version published in New Zealand five years previously, as discussed by McDonald in Chapter 5, this volume).

While others have focused on the "truth" (or "fiction") of Ashton-Warner's tales of conflicts with convention and authority, my intention has been to locate her educational theory within the conceptual landscapes, or linguistic spaces, of her place and time. But such analyses work at the level of abstraction and, unlike most educational theorists, Sylvia did not write in abstractions, but rather expressed her educational philosophy through diary entries, novels and poetic imagery. Intensely personal, her educational writing is incandescent with images of place. In Sylvia's textual images of hills and pathways, houses and classrooms it is possible to discern faint trails connecting her secluded schoolrooms, shacks and houses with wider metropolitan networks of educational thought.

Sylvia's place: Sheds, schools, rivers and bridges

Just after the start of World War Two, Sylvia and Keith Henderson moved from an isolated East Coast Native School (Horoera) to Pipiriki, high up the Whanganui River. Her autobiographical book *Myself* is replete with spatial images. Their new classroom had a "tall ceiling, high rafters and a lot of air and echoes" (*Myself*, 1967b, p. 60). Bachelard (2002, p. 6), the philosopher, writes that "an entire past comes to dwell in a new house", and Sylvia sensed a "frightening Inspector shade in the rafters, limiting and aborting all I do" (*Spinster*, 1958, p. 190). Her mother had been a teacher, struggling through World War One and the Depression to support an invalid husband and 10 children. With continual "Inspector troubles", the family was always on the move. As a child, Sylvia attended 10 small schools, usually taught by her mother.

In some of Sylvia's texts, inspectors are cast as the allies of New Education that 1940s policies intended them to become. But in others, inspectors are phantoms, shades of their punitive force in her childhood: "There's a ghoul from the past that haunts, I think, all teachers of my generation, from those five-year-old days when we felt the tension of the teacher and the foreboding of the Inspector himself" (*Teacher*, 1963, p. 198). While the isolation of her previous school, Horoera, had precipitated her "nervous breakdown", she'd had freedom there, "far from the haunts of inspectors". In Pipiriki, "with roads and bridges and no tidal rivers, an inspector could walk in any day" (*Myself*, 1967b, p. 67). Like the houses in Bachelard's account, for Sylvia the schoolroom was a primal space for "thoughts, memories and dreams ... The binding principle in this integration is the daydream. Past, present and future give the house different dynamisms, which often interfere, at times opposing, at time stimulating one another" (Bachelard, 2002, p. 26).

But war was a greater outside threat: "We laughed a great deal ... until Pearl Harbour" (*Myself*, 1967b, p. 60). Domestic routines accommodated War Institute meetings, Keith's Home Guard duties, a sister who "arrived from the capital where her home is between three targets just asking for Japanese bombs" (p. 61). Sylvia read Freud's *Introductory Lectures*, and formulated her theory of violence: "The word beginning with a capital V widespread across the world. The violence I believe to be in all of us is subdued in the undermind, waiting, but which blasts out on occasion depending on how near the surface it is, or on the rigidity of the surface" (*Teacher*, 1963, p. 32). The "design" of her work, the key vocabulary scheme, was "that creativity in this time of life when character can be influenced for ever is the solution to the problem of war" (Sylvia, 1956a, p. 295). While policy suggested teachers act as a "buffer" between children and war, Sylvia took the lid off repressed fears. In *Myself*, she outlined her theory to a visiting inspector

> I suppose that schools in the big city slums ... If I were teaching there I ... And if I were allowed to I ... I mean children from criminal homes, starved and that. Throats cut in the night and that sort of thing,

> hungry, stealing ... I'd give them words like "knife" and "cutthroat" and ... "jail" and "police" and "blood". I'd give them words they lived with.
>
> "Words they lived with," repeated Mr Harrison.
>
> But he only repeated the last phrase, not stepping forward. It seemed as though he were stalled. "See, what I mean is," I go on, "I'd relate through words the outside of a child to the inside of a child and then you'd get integration." (*Myself*, 1967b, p. 110)

While Sylvia tried to explain that repressed violence inside young children needs release, the inspector was distracted by matters outside

> "The thing to do," flash of hands, "is to give them bad books like themselves, then you'd integrate them, then you'd get them peaceful."
>
> "Then you'd get them peaceful," indulgently, "I say," Mr Henderson, eyes out the door, "where's that spot where you plan to dig a trench for the children? There's no telling when we're going to get this visit from the Pacific. Under the pines over there?"
>
> "Impracticable. You can't dig through the roots. No, Mr Harrison, I plan it nearer the school, just at the edge of the playground there." (*Myself*, 1967b, p. 110)

While Sylvia, inside her classroom, theorises about violence in the child's inner world, the men focus on the outer world, planning a trench through the school grounds for protection against violence in the form of an air attack.

Sylvia requires a separate house for her dreaming: "no voices and no doors banging. No pace, no demand for answers ... and no war news" (*Myself*, 1967b, p. 74). From an early age, she dreamed of being elsewhere. Bachelard writes, "It is on the plane of the daydream and not on that of facts that childhood remains alive and poetically useful within us" (2002, p. 16). In *Myself*, Sylvia describes

> bleakly counting my bead-dreams that I dreamed when I was single about how I would live my life: a glamorous mysterious vivid life in the capitals of the world with those of my own kind—artists, musicians and writers. And lovers demanding a look from me, and friends thinking me wonderful. Paris, Rome, New York... roaming, roaming, fascinated. Getting on and off ships and trains and planes, the last word in fashion. Without remembering those dreams and seeing them against what I am now: a forgotten girl on the top of a hill drearily teaching Maoris. A forgotten girl. (*Myself*, 1967b, p. 20)

Glamour, excitement, art and romance are "over there", in cities she has never seen, where the authors of the books she reads live and work. What and where she is "now" (on a hill "teaching Maoris") means oblivion, being "forgotten" (invisible) to people she has never met, but desires to become.

To highlight the "New Zealandness" of Ashton-Warner's theoretical writing, it is useful to place the above extract alongside one by a very differently located woman writer. A generation older than Ashton-Warner, Virginia Woolf was born in London into an intellectual middle-class family. As an adult, Woolf lived the bohemian intellectual, artistic and sexual freedom of Ashton-Warner's daydreams. In the following account, Woolf evokes the Hyde Park house where she had lived as a child

> The tea table rather than the dinner table was the centre of Victorian family life—in our family at least. Savages I suppose have some tree, or fire place around which they congregate; the round table marked that focal, that sacred spot in the house. It was the centre, the heart of the family. It was the centre to which the sons returned from their work in the evening; the hearth whose fire was tended by the mother, pouring out tea. In the same way, the bedroom—the double bedded bedroom on the first floor was the sexual centre, the birth centre, the death centre of the house. (Woolf, 2002, p. 125)

Woolf wrote: "The division in our life was curious. Downstairs there was pure convention, upstairs pure intellect. But the there was no connection between them" (p. 158). With the help of servants, the mother's (downstairs) work involved care of the body, presiding over the fire, pouring tea for returning sons, performing social rituals demanded by Victorian convention. Upstairs, cut off from such menial concerns, was her "father's great study ... entirely booklined ... the brain of the house" (p. 125). Only the bedroom connected the two: babies, and death. The floor plan was vertical, segmented by gender.

The spatiality of Sylvia's life "on top of a hill" was more untamed. Initially she accommodated her personae as teacher, wife, mother, lover, artist and writer in domestic space by demarcations of time

> I have so much to do between school and home that I have to give every minute its value. I must keep my reading and learning of poetry going and mental exercises; Huxley, Russell and such, from the public library, the new book clubs; one book at least has been suitable: *This Hill Is Mine*. Also there is the Maori language to continue learning, schoolwork, scheme, workbook and chart preparation. I practice Maori sentences that Mrs Hira has taught me; over and over again, whenever I am alone, doing dishes and sweeping. Whenever I rest I pick up my novel and last thing at night I read one poem.
>
> I do my school work in the afternoon and after tea. I paint charts in the conglomerate sun porch, but still there's a book to be written; every night, dead or dying, after school work and letters, I get in those few lines. (*Myself*, 1967b, p. 28)

The policy of "cultural integration" (learning Māori language) was performed while sweeping; state-supported access to good literature in rural areas (through book clubs and libraries) enhanced her evening study; family space (in the sun porch) was shared with the making of visual classroom resources advocated by the New Education. "In place of an imagination of a world of bounded places," writes Doreen Massey, "we are now presented with a world of flows. Instead of isolated identities, an understanding of the spatial as relational through connections" (2005, p. 81).

Sylvia dreams of a separate place for creativity, removed from school and family. She rents a shack, calling it "Selah". Sylvia writes: "Selah is the house I've built before in the brilliance of wistful fantasy, emerging into reality. This is the geography of it. Here could be the fresh air of independence, the miracle of solitude ... of music, study and painting" (*Myself*, 1967b, p. 116). Bohemian Europe might pass that way: "Elegant people will come with their hair quietly parted. Terrific conversations plunging through till morning ..." Like other rooms in Sylvia's psyche, this shack was haunted: shadows of a murder-suicide of two young (Māori) lovers there. She imagines "pretty curtains blowing the dead away" (*Myself*, 1967b, p. 116). Can she claim this space for art? Sylvia's own ghosts and ghouls follow: "I've always seen the artist as a monster coming in from the outside that inhabited my brain, my mind, quite distinct from me. I couldn't have the monster in the family." Accordingly, "I locked the artist away in the study. I locked him out. I had to go to him."[13] Selah must contain the demons of her undermind—her dreams, illicit passions, and the writing that disciplined dreaming. The mad woman looms in the garret: "Asylums are full of artists who failed to say the things they must, and famous tombs with those who did" (*Incense to Idols*, 1960, p. 169).

In the quotations cited earlier, Sylvia called out to her readers from high "on a hill teaching Maoris". On the other side of the world, Virginia Woolf looked back into her childhood's domestic interiors. Writing from "inside" the metropolitan centre, Woolf speculated that "savages" (colonial "others") might orient their lives spatially around "some tree or fire place". But savages were distant figures of Woolf's imagination, remote from the orderly Victorian rooms in which ladies poured tea and men speculated upstairs in book-lined studies. Positioned geographically in Woolf's antipodes, Sylvia could only dream of "a glamorous mysterious vivid life in the capitals of the

---

13 Transcribed from television interview with Jack Shallcrass (Barnett, 1978).

world". Woolf's metropolis is Sylvia's imaginary; Sylvia's open spaces, and her hill among "Maoris", Woolf's. Located on opposite sides of the imperial divide, both writers echoed the tropes of race: Empire, metropolis/periphery, civilisation and savagery (Maloney, 2001).

As Cathryn McConaghy has argued, "Sylvia constructed her notion of race usually within the tropes of the day" (2006, p. 74). Consistent with policies of her time, Sylvia's teaching scheme was not intended to promote what today is referred to as biculturalism (or bilingualism). It was designed as "a bridge from the known to the unknown; from a native culture to a new; and universally speaking, from the inner man out" (*Teacher*, 1963, p. 28). The key-words scheme, which tapped inner (psychic) dimensions of the child's mind, was a transition: "They can't bridge the gap between the pa and the European school without it" (*Spinster*, 1958, p. 115). Failure to cross over (into civilisation) meant going "back" to nature (savagery)

> The transition made by Maori children is often unsuccessful. At a tender age a wrench occurs from one culture to another, from which either manifestly or unconsciously, not all recover. And I think that this circumstance has some little bearing on the number of Maoris who, although well educated, seem neurotic, and on the number who retreat to the mat. (*Teacher*, 1963, p. 31)

Sylvia's image of "back to the mat" was a recurring one in racial discourse. Professor Fitt (cited previously) used it: "… the main outcome of our attempts to educate the Maori has been failure. That this is so is substantiated by the reports from so many competent observers that the one longing of so many Maori boys and girls, once their schooling is over, is to 'return to the mat', that is, to the old paternal ways of living" (1931, p. 223). In *Bell Call*, Ashton-Warner refers to "Some secluded spot, some overlooked Maori pa where … children can merge with nature" (1971, p. 27). And in her novel *Greenstone*, Huia, a child of mixed race, crosses back and forth across the river between "This" (it's/her Pākehā) side and "That" (it's/her Māori) side:

> As the canoe makes its nervous way across the ponderously moving water her inner world changes colour and character. That Side is everything that is Maori, This Side in the clearing all that is English, each side demanding its inherited loyalty, while right here on the treacherous surface of the river is the recurring transition … this sundering feeling accompanying movement from one race to another. Where can her spirit fly like a bird to its nest where conflict is forgotten? (1967a, p. 129)

As Tess Moeke-Maxwell (2006) suggests, *Greenstone*'s evocations of rivers, canoes, bridges, transitions and hybridity evoke theoretical engagement with policies of cultural fusion. Sylvia makes few references to Māori culture in her teaching (apart from the children's key words), and her arts are European: The Pied Piper mural, the European classical music she played on "the new piano ... Here was this Friedman in a Maori schoolroom" (*Myself*, 1967b, p. 31) (see Penfold and Tawhiwhirangi, Chapter 8 and 9, this volume, on lack of Māori language in Sylvia's classrooms).

Conclusion

To locate Sylvia Ashton-Warner as a New Zealand educational theorist, the "localisation in the spaces of our intimacy is more urgent than determination of dates" (Bachelard, 2002, p. 50). We create our "selves", or identities, in particular social, geographical and cultural settings. Sylvia Henderson, a teacher in a Native School, dreamed and wrote her persona as Sylvia Ashton-Warner, novelist and educational theorist, in (and not in spite of) Pipiriki during World War Two. The places in which she lived, dreamed, read, thought, loved and wrote should not be seen as isolated cells or containers. Studying Sylvia Ashton-Warner as a *New Zealand* educational theorist—knowing her place—reveals connections between her haunted hills, classrooms and houses and wider metropolitan movements of educational thought.

References

Abbiss, J. (1998). The 'New Education Fellowship' in New Zealand: Its activity and influence in the 1930s and 1940s. *New Zealand Journal of Educational Studies, 33*(1), 81–93.

Ashton-Warner, S. (1958). *Spinster*. London: Secker & Warburg.

Ashton-Warner, S. (1960). *Incense to idols*. London: Secker & Warburg.

Ashton-Warner, S. (1963). *Teacher*. New York: Simon & Schuster.

Ashton-Warner, S. (1967a). *Greenstone*. Christchurch: Whitcombe & Tombs.

Ashton-Warner, S. (1967b). *Myself*. New York: Simon & Schuster.

Ashton-Warner, S. (1971). *Bell call*. Christchurch: Whitcombe & Tombs.

Ashton-Warner, S. (1979/1980). *I passed this way*. Wellington: Reed.

Atmore, H. (1929). Report of the Minister of Education. In *Appendices to the Journal of the House of Representatives* (E1).

Bachelard, G. (2002). *The poetics of space* (M. Jolas, Trans.). Boston, MA: Beacon Press. (Original work published 1994)

Ball, D. (1936). Report of the Senior Inspector of Native Schools. In *Appendices to the Journal of the House of Representatives* (E3).

Ball, D. C. (1939). Report of the Senior Inspector of Native Schools. In *Appendices to the Journal of the House of Representatives* (E3).

Barnett, J. (Producer). (1978). *Three New Zealanders: Sylvia Ashton-Warner* [Television programme]. Wellington: Endeavour Films.

Barrington, J. (1987). The Maori schools: A fresh perspective. In R. Openshaw & D. McKenzie (Eds.), *Reinterpreting the educational past* (pp. 168–180). Wellington: New Zealand Council for Educational Research.

Barrington, J. (2008). *Separate but equal?: Maori schools and the Crown, 1867–1969*. Wellington: Victoria University Press.

Barrington, J., & Beaglehole, T. (1974). *Maori schools in a changing society*. Wellington: New Zealand Council for Educational Research.

Beeby, C. E. (1992). *Biography of an idea: Beeby on education*. Wellington: New Zealand Council for Educational Research.

Caldwell Cook, H. (1917). *The play way*. London: Heinemann

Campbell, A. E. (Ed.). (1938). *Modern trends in education: Proceedings of the New Zealand NEF conference*. Wellington: Whitcombe and Tombs.

Clemens, S. (1996). *Pay attention to the children: Lessons for teachers and parents from Sylvia Ashton-Warner*. Napa, CA: Rattle OK Publications.

Department of Education. (1929). *Syllabus of instruction for public schools* [the "Red Book"]. Wellington: Government Printer.

Dewey, J. (1916). *Democracy and education*. New York: MacMillan.

Fletcher, T. A. (1948). Report of the Chief Inspector of Maori Schools. In *Appendices to the Journal of the House of Representatives* (E3).

Fitt, A. G. (1931). Racial contacts: Some problems of Maori children. In P. M. Jackson (Ed.), *Maori and education* (pp. 220–229). Wellington: Ferguson & Osborn.

Gibbons, P. (2003). The far side of the search for identity: Reconsidering New Zealand history. *New Zealand Journal of History*, 37(1), 1–10.

Grumet, M. (1988). *Bitter milk: Women and teaching*. Amherst, MA: University of Massachusetts Press.

Hood, L. (1988). *Sylvia! The biography of Sylvia Ashton-Warner*. Auckland: Viking.

Isaacs, S. (1938). The principle of activity in modern education. In A. E. Campbell (Ed.), *Modern trends in education: Proceedings of the New Zealand NEF conference* (p. 504). Wellington: Whitcombe and Tombs.

Jackson, P. M. (Ed.). (1931). *Maori and education*. Wellington: Ferguson & Osborn.

Lopdell, F. C. (1952). Report of the Chief Inspector of Primary Schools. In *Appendices to the Journal of the House of Representatives* (E2).

Maloney, P. (2001). Savagery and civilisation: Early Victorian notions. *New Zealand Journal of History*, 35(2), 153–156.

Mason, H. R. G. (1940). Report of the Minister of Education. In *Appendices to the Journal of the House of Representatives* (E1).

Massey, D. (2005). *For space*. London: Sage.

May, H. (2003). *Discovery of early childhood*. Wellington: Bridget Williams Books.

McConaghy, C. (2006). Teaching's intimacies. In J. Robertson & C. McConaghy (Eds.), *Provocations: Sylvia Ashton-Warner and excitability in education* (pp. 63–94). New York: Peter Lang.

Middleton, S. (2006). "I my own professor": Ashton-Warner as New Zealand educational theorist 1940–1960. In J. Robertson & C. McConaghy (Eds.), *Provocations: Sylvia Ashton-Warner and excitability in education* (pp. 37–55). New York: Peter Lang.

Middleton, S., & May, H. (1997). *Teachers talk teaching 1915–1995: Early childhood, schools and teachers' colleges*. Palmerston North: Dunmore Press.

Moeke-Maxwell, T. (2006). InSide/outSide cultural hybridity: *Greenstone* as narrative provocateur. In J. Robertson & C. McConaghy (Eds.), *Provocations: Sylvia Ashton-Warner and excitability in education* (pp. 95–117). New York: Peter Lang.

Neill, A. S. (1968). *Summerhill*. Harmondsworth: Penguin.

Overton, G. E. (1945). Report of the Chief Inspector of Primary Schools. In *Appendices to the Journal of the House of Representatives* (E2).

Read, H. (1958). *Education through art*. London: Faber.

Reports of the Minister of Education (1928–1956). In *Appendices to the Journal of the House of Representatives* (E1).

Reports of the Chief Inspectors of Primary Schools (1928–1956). In *Appendices to the Journal of the House of Representatives* (E2).

Reports of the Chief Inspectors of Native Schools. (1928-1956). In *Appendices to the Journal of the House of Representatives* (E3)..

Simon, J. (Ed.). (1998). *Ngā kura Māori: The native schools system 1867-1969*. Auckland: Auckland University Press.

Simon, J., & Tuhiwai Smith, L. (Eds.). (2001). *A civilising mission? Perceptions and representations of the Native Schools system*. Auckland: Auckland University Press.

Simpson, G. (1974). Participation in the Northern Maori project. In D. Bray & C. Hill (Eds.), *Polynesian and Pakeha in New Zealand education Vol. 2: Ethnic difference and the school* (pp. 94–98). Auckland: Heinemann Educational Books.

Somerset, G. (1988). *Sunshine and shadow*. Auckland: New Zealand Playcentre Federation.

Stubbs, G. H. (1943). Report of the Senior Inspector of Native Schools. In *Appendices to the Journal of the House of Representatives*.

Sylvia. (1956a, 3 September). Organic teaching: The unlived life. *National Education, 414*, 294–295.

Sylvia. (1956b, 1 February). The Maori Infant Room: No. 2: Private Key Vocabularies. *National Education, 407*, 10–12.

Sylvia. (1956c, 1 October). Tone. *National Education, 415*, 342–343.

Woolf, V. (2002). *Moments of being: Autobiographical writings*. London: Random House.

Author

Sue Middleton is a professor of education at the University of Waikato. She has an interest in the lives and works of New Zealand educational theorists; in particular, women teachers who were also writers (such as Sylvia Ashton-Warner), and how their educational ideas were enabled and constrained by their historical circumstances. Her books include: *Disciplining Sexuality: Foucault, Life-histories and Education; Teachers Talk Teaching 1915–1995: Early Childhood, Schools, and Teachers' Colleges; Women and Education in Aotearoa*.
Email: educ_mid@waikato.ac.nz

CHAPTER 4

Far too original: Sylvia Ashton-Warner's novels and her complicated relationship with New Zealand

Emily Dobson

Emily Dobson, a New Zealand literary scholar, examines Sylvia Ashton-Warner's status in New Zealand literature, and explores two of her lesser known novels: *Incense to Idols* and *Bell Call*.

Sylvia Ashton-Warner's name is not often heard these days. Students of New Zealand literature have no idea who she is, though university lecturers have a half-remembered awareness of her and teachers may have the odd copy of *Spinster* or *Teacher* tucked away at the back of the bookshelf. The name occasionally resurfaces, as it did when her house, "Whenua", came up for sale in 1998 ("Author's 'Heaven'", 1998), and, more significantly, in C. K. Stead's revised collection of essays, *Kin of Place* (2002). For the most part, however, her place in our national consciousness seems to have steadily faded towards obscurity. Ironically, if she is known at all today, it is more likely for not being sufficiently acknowledged. Many critics point out that she "received recognition and status overseas, but not in her own country" (Jones, 1990, p. 331), yet offer little beyond this statement.

It is also overwhelmingly as an educator, not a writer, that she is remembered. In 1961, Joan Stevens pointed out that the "vigorous discussion" surrounding *Spinster* focused on biographical details, noting that "its very authenticity led readers astray, in the manner so characteristic of us, into judging the novel as a transcript of fact". She concluded that "too many discussions of *Spinster* ignore its creative aspects" (p. 103). The crossover between educational nonfiction and creative fiction in Ashton-Warner's work, along with her dual role as teacher and writer, undoubtedly contributed to an underestimation of her status as a writer. In 1980, Jack Shallcrass made the particularly accurate prediction that "it is as a teacher that she is known and will be remembered" (p. 68). Michael Firth's 1985 film *Sylvia* reiterated the sentimental image of an artist of inspired genius, working passionately amid a flock of Māori children and struggling against a rigid and oppressive authority. This image of Ashton-Warner, which probably helped to increase her popularity overseas during the height of her success, easily provokes skepticism today. Indeed, even in the year the film was made, Ashton-Warner's ideas on teaching were being cited as "abhorrent cultural elitism" (Rountree & Williams, 1985, p. 64).

Contribution to literature

Ashton-Warner's most significant contribution is arguably not in education but in literature, in the form of a magnificent autobiography, *I Passed This Way* (1979/1980) that won the nonfiction section of the 1980 New Zealand Book Awards. This text displays her writing skills at their most breathtaking, and offers a remarkable insight into the bizarre upbringing that had such an influence on her unique perception of the world. It also created something of a cult around her eccentric, idiosyncratic personality, which was strengthened with the publication of Lynley Hood's celebrated biography in 1988.

However, Ashton-Warner should not be remembered only as a teacher or the writer of an impressive autobiography. Between 1958 and 1972, in addition to her two creatively written teaching books—*Teacher* (1963) and *Spearpoint: Teacher in America* (1972)—and an autobiographical novel, *Myself* (1967), she published five novels: *Spinster* (1958), *Incense to Idols* (1960), *Bell Call* (1964), *Greenstone* (1966) and *Three* (1970).

All of these novels have enormous scope for reinvestigation. Aside from the sheer quality of the writing—which displays an impressive and strikingly modern economic style, a deep understanding of relationships, sharp sense of humour and a particularly brilliant flair for dialogue—the novels can also provide a sparkling alternative to the regionalism that until recently has dominated New Zealand literature. And yet, despite the foreign protagonists, unantipodean indulgences and global awareness, New Zealand has an unquestionably strong presence in Ashton-Warner's work. The novels can be read as revealing something about the New Zealand artist and their place within this country.

This chapter, then, has two objectives. The first is to examine Ashton-Warner's status within New Zealand literature by mapping the development of critical responses to her work. The second is to explore two novels: *Incense to Idols*, and, more briefly, *Bell Call*. In reaction against the typical focus on either Ashton-Warner's work as a teacher or the circumstances of her life, this selection is particular. Educational and explicitly autobiographical work is deliberately avoided. *Incense to Idols* is of particular interest, as it seems dramatically to have put Ashton-Warner out of favour with many leading New Zealand critics. *Bell Call* is worthy of attention in its own right. Like *Three,* this fascinating and well-written novel appears to have been undeservedly ignored in the wake of *Incense to Idols'* dubious reception.

Part One: Locating Ashton-Warner within New Zealand literature: "She's out in the pines writing sentimental piffle"[1]

Emerging around the same time as Janet Frame's *Owls do Cry* (1957), Ian Cross' *The God Boy* (1958) and M. K. Joseph's *I'll Soldier No More* (1958), Ashton-Warner's first novel *Spinster* (1958) was hailed as part of an exciting new wave of New Zealand fiction. E. H. McCormick described these four texts as "novels of marked distinction" (1959, p. 161), and Charles Brasch found "favourable signs in the acceptance by British publishers of unapologetically New Zealand novels" (cited in Jones, 1991, p. 141). At this point Ashton-Warner was clearly an author of significance and potential equaling that of Frame and Cross: figures who, unlike Ashton-Warner, have come to be of immense importance to New Zealand literature. A decade later, Winston Rhodes was still referring to "the acknowledged mastery of Sylvia Ashton-Warner, Janet Frame and Frank Sargeson" (1969, p. 7).

Spinster was particularly anticipated because it had received highly favourable responses overseas before being released here. Joan Stevens commented that "it was read therefore here with great interest, and promptly became the centre of vigorous discussion" (1961, p. 103). The fact that Ashton-Warner seemed to have come out

---

1 "So whenever Mama demanded, 'Where's Sylvie?' Daphne's standard reply was, 'She's out in the pines writing sentimental piffle.'" (Hood, 1988, p. 27).

of nowhere merely fuelled the fires, and Dennis McEldowney noted in 1969 that "*Spinster* in 1958 was unforeseen. That was part of the reason for the excitement that greeted it" (1969, p. 241). According to Lynley Hood, *Spinster* was "more discussed and praised in the media than any previous New Zealand novel" (1988, p. 157).

The excitement generated by *Spinster*'s overseas release and acclaim was a two-sided coin, however. Despite the simple reality that *Spinster* was "rejected locally" (Gibbons, 1991, p. 92), publishing overseas may have resulted in the critical sentiment that Ashton-Warner was betraying her own nation's literary interests, an attitude typified by Allen Curnow's rigorous nationalism. C. K. Stead has commented that "it was something in the literature of the 1940s and fifties which called itself 'international' that Curnow particularly set himself against" (1981b, p. 140). In his 1963 essay "New Zealand Literature: The Case for a Working Definition", Curnow described the problem of "literary emulation" in the New Zealand writer, whose "trouble" was that "he *reads* too much [...] and he imports nearly all he reads" (1987, p. 203). "Success of this sort", he elaborated,

> is a low ambition, by which I mean an inadequate, not a despicable one. It is the kind of success most generally expected by New Zealanders of their writers, and invariably gets the best press. (1987, p. 203)

Indeed, Curnow continued his essay by wondering whether

> writers like Miss Frame, Mr Ian Cross, Miss Ashton-Warner and Mr Maurice Shadbolt measure their success by the current notice their fictions have won abroad, or by the permanent place they may have in what we must call 'New Zealand Literature'? I am guessing, but I would be surprised if the former were not the case. (1987, p. 204)

Similarly, there is a subtle sense of resentment in Stevens' comment that "*Spinster* was published in England, where it attracted rave reviews before New Zealanders ever had a chance to get their hands on it" (1961, p. 103). *Spinster*'s foreign protagonist, Miss

Anna Vorontosov, did not help the situation, and critics such as the *Listener*'s David Hall were quick to complain that "it is never clear why this novel's heroine has to be so untypical" (1958, p. 12). Curnow criticised Ashton-Warner sharply for this, arguing that

> there is something starved and formless about the novel where characters lack precise orientation within a world whose limits are known ... The case of Miss Vorontosov is exemplary. She comes from nowhere. Wherever she belongs it is not where she is. (1987, p. 268)

Criticisms like these sprang from, and added to, a growing mutual resentment between Ashton-Warner and her country. The rejection of *Spinster* by local publishers was incorporated into the author's "powerful need for rejection" that "recurred again and again as an unspoken driving force in her life" (Hood, 1988, p. 121). This sense of persecution, the development of which is perceptively outlined in Hood's biography, fuelled Ashton-Warner's increasingly caustic criticism of New Zealand's oppressive society. *Spinster*'s foreign protagonist was undoubtedly a result of Ashton-Warner's distaste for the average New Zealander. She became known for her particularly vehement hatred of New Zealand, setting herself up as one "who's been both rejected by and who has rejected my country" (Ashton-Warner, cited in Hood, 1988, p. 247). This feeling of rejection was nurtured, primarily, by Ashton-Warner herself. The extreme difficulties involved in working with her, along with her dedicated avoidance of "the approbations being showered upon her", ensured that "invitations dried to a trickle and she was able to settle back into her favourite role of neglected genius" (1988, p. 158). The consequences of this vigorous personal conflict are noted in Hood's observation that "The New Zealand literary community responded to the general disillusionment with Sylvia by downplaying the significance of Sylvia Ashton-Warner's writing" (1988, p. 185).

Predictably, critics also accused *Spinster* of displaying stylistic deficiencies conventionally associated with women's writing.

Reviewers complained about the novel's "occasional self-consciousness" (Hall, 1958, p. 12), "almost hysterical monologue" and "woolly catchwords" (Munro, 1958, pp. 280–1). If these were softened with the modifiers *occasional* and *almost*, the publication of *Incense to Idols* inspired critics to really go to town. Paul Day memorably declared that "Germaine de Bauvais [the central character in *Incense to Idols*] […] emerges not as a woman but as a preposterous series of bogus attitudes, a magazine-reader's fantasy of high fashion, sophistication and sin" (1961, p. 91). Joan Stevens described "Germaine's undisciplined flood of sensations" (1961, p. 107). The accusations were similar to those that plagued Robin Hyde in the 1930s, exemplified in Frank Sargeson's comment to Denis Glover that "I've told [Robin] bluntly that being hysterical on paper isn't writing" (cited in Murray, 1998, p. 166). It didn't help that *Incense to Idols* featured another artistic foreigner, with a "general distaste for small-town New Zealand" (Hall, 1960, p. 12). Even Dennis McEldowney, in the most comprehensive investigation of Ashton-Warner's writing of the time, thought that "in adopting the persona of a French pianist […] she has taken on something for which she is not equipped" (1969, p. 240).

Turning point

Although ranked by *Time* magazine as among the five best works of fiction for that year (Hood, 1984, p. 24), an honour *Spinster* had also received, *Incense to Idols* was arguably the critical turning point for Ashton-Warner's status as a writer in New Zealand. While *Spinster* would always warrant attention in terms of its revelations for the educational world and its "compulsive realism of the classroom" (Day, 1961, p. 91), the general consensus seems to have been that *Incense to Idols* had rocketed beyond serious New Zealand literary endeavour.

In his 1969 essay, McEldowney noticed the unfortunate sequence of Ashton-Warner's novels, commenting that

> although [*Incense to Idols*] was hardly a book one could ignore, it did seem possible that Miss Ashton-Warner had shot her bolt with *Spinster* [...]. Her next book, *Teacher* (1963), appeared to confirm this view. It was assembled from the material which had gone into *Spinster*, and made her claim as an educator rather than a writer. This opinion is still widely held, because the novel which followed, *Bell Call* (1964), is the least well-known of her books in her own country. (p. 241)

This certainly seems to be the case. With the exception of McEldowney's essay, Ashton-Warner virtually disappeared from the pages of *Landfall*, then New Zealand's leading literary magazine, until an "In Memoriam" in 1984. Even this was somewhat farcical, since most of the article was transferred verbatim from an earlier review of *I Passed This Way* written for the *Listener*. The new material consisted of (posthumously appropriate) exaggerated gushing, which even then conspicuously ignored everything between *Teacher* and *I Passed This Way*. The article concluded with an optimistic, if unfulfilled, prediction that "[Ashton-Warner's] writing will be in the thick of it for many years, in many places" (Shallcrass, 1984, p. 344). For it is really only *Spinster*, a "minor classic", and *I Passed This Way*, that attract any attention at all today. It seems likely that *Spinster*, "a sensation at the time of its publication [...] still tends to eclipse the author's succeeding novels" (Jones & Jones, 1983, p. 49).

Despite *Landfall*'s cessation of interest in Ashton-Warner, her novels continued to be reviewed in the *Listener*. These reviews often draw attention to aspects of the intriguing development of New Zealand's attitude towards Ashton-Warner's writing and personality. To his credit, David Hall examined *Teacher* as a creative work and not just an educational manual, despite the characteristic remark that "there is more emotion than meat". The review concludes favourably, situating the work firmly in a national context as "a book intensely individual yet sensitive to the flavour of life in this country and full of dedication and spirit" (1963, p. 19).

Hall's greater reservations about Ashton-Warner's next novel, *Greenstone*, included a criticism that would play a key part in Ashton-Warner's increasing unpopularity: that although she was

> creditably willing to strike a blow for interracial harmony [...] the direct invocation of the romanticism of Maori culture is about as effective as the same sort of material invoked in the flaccid lines of Alfred Domett. (1968, p. 21)

This view looks ahead to the 1980s, when Michael King, in the same review that advocated a reinvestigation of Robin Hyde's novels, described the Māori component of Ashton-Warner's writing as "dated", "gauche and naive", "patronising" and "embarrassing" (1986, p. 160). These criticisms fail to recognise something that McEldowney had gestured towards in 1969—that while

> the Maori theme and Maori myth is romanticised in a way it would indeed have been done in the 'twenties, in which the book is set [...] The structure [...] is far more artful and allusive than any writer would have achieved at the time (1969, p. 244).

References to Māori

References to Māori in Ashton-Warner's writing have been consistently misunderstood from a variety of viewpoints. For example, Joan Stevens (1961, p. 105) declared that *Spinster* was "*not a novel about how to educate Maori children*". David Hall (1963, p. 18) saw *Teacher* within a tradition in which "Maori naturalness and dignity are superior to European prissiness". Winston Rhodes, with the patronising tone that Ashton-Warner herself has been accused of, claimed that

> the most impressive aspects of Sylvia Ashton-Warner's *Spinster* are concerned with [...] the warm humanity of the infant room in a Maori school where relationships and ways of living are revealed in an atmosphere of love and understanding. (1969, p. 36)

Bill Pearson located *Spinster* within the "very recent development" (in 1958) of stories which involve

> brief chance meetings with Maoris by writers who, because they distrust sentimental preconceptions of the Maoris, simply observe and record with a sympathetic detachment, not cold, but not warm either, nor very informed. (1958, p. 231)

Ashton-Warner's writing fits none of these descriptions particularly well. *Spinster* is, among other things, a novel about how to educate Māori children. "Maori naturalness" is not always constructed as being superior to "European prissiness": the narrator of *Teacher* often prefers the European children simply because they are her own kind. Violent feelings and racial tensions frequently contradict Rhodes' "atmosphere of love and understanding". And yet Ashton-Warner was neither detached from the Māori children in her school, nor from the Māori community. She was in fact rather well informed. Lynley Hood tells us that at Pipiriki

> Sylvia immersed herself in Maori culture [...] She became a fluent Maori speaker and enjoyed animated conversations with the old people who spoke no English at all. She addressed gatherings of school parents in Maori [...] She also studied Maori art and crafts: she soaked flax in mud and made her own piupiu [reed skirts]; she kept an outside fire going for days under a big iron pot to make Maori peanuts from karaka berries; she ate lamprey eels and pork bones with puha; she learnt to dry whitebait in summer and preserve meat in fat; she even drank Mai's home-brew. (1988, pp. 100–101)

Any writing about a native people by a European risks being seen as colonial narrative, and of being accused as such. It may be that, in terms of racial understanding, Ashton-Warner was in many ways still a product of her time, in which case we would need to accept this and look beyond it to the genuine quality of the writing. But it does seem that she simply wasn't bothered by such delicate cultural correctness. Her references to Māori are as complex and as seemingly contradictory as the woman herself. An entirely different paper could be written on the Māori component of her writing—there has not yet been an adequate investigation of it.

Public profile

The 1969 review of Ashton-Warner's next book, *Myself*, was notable in terms of what it said about Ashton-Warner's public profile at the time. The review, by Jack Shallcrass, was accompanied by a large photo and began, "There can be few New Zealanders who will come to this book without some knowledge of the author … A substantial number will have read her work." It then described how Ashton-Warner was well known for her success, "which we now clutch at possessively". The review had an overwhelmingly positive tone, and, significantly, a rare positive slant on emotion in the novel, as Shallcrass asserted that "it is easier to function, as most of us do, in the middle of the spectrum of feeling but it is exhilarating to meet, if only on paper, someone who goes off the top of the scale." He also managed to implicate Ashton-Warner in a kind of idealised Frame-ian tradition, where "some of her difficulties arose from her painful shyness and lack of security" (1969, p. 16).

The identification of Ashton-Warner with Frame, and also Katherine Mansfield, was expounded more intelligently by C. K. Stead in 1981. Stead referred to McEldowney's 1969 essay, which looked at the "feminine" tradition in New Zealand and its "problem of grounding"—that is, the problem of finding a suitable format for expressing emotion. Stead argued beyond this idea to assert that

> In the writing of each at its best there is clarity of vision, an uncommitted intelligence, a capacity both for passion and detachment; and the detachment is never far removed from a sense of comedy that is a form of revolt against all prevailing pieties. (1981a, p. 52)

Referring to Stead's essay, Lawrence Jones then also situated Ashton-Warner within a "'feminine', subjective, impressionistic tradition" (1990, p. 332). Jones, writing on Ashton-Warner's autobiography, followed what had become a common trend by viewing her writing in the context of a repressive New Zealand society. In this view New Zealand is characterised by

> [a] distrust of emotion, [a] lack of respect for the aesthetic, [a] restriction of opportunity and accomplishment for women, and [an] authoritarian control of non-conformity. (1990, p. 331)

This was, of course, something that Ashton-Warner herself believed with intense conviction and made explicit in her autobiography. The issue had been the focal point of Shallcrass' 1980 review of *I Passed This Way*, in which he wrote that "someone who sees the world from the inside is a source of unease to a culture as aggressively external and physical as ours", and claimed that Ashton-Warner had "found herself at war with her own practical and not always imaginative countrymen" (p. 68).

Around this time, one can detect the developing critical perception of Ashton-Warner as it began to solidify. Seen by a few as a kind of hero and martyr, she was characterised particularly by a sense of animosity and unorthodoxy. At the same time, her public profile was steadily and quietly diminishing. Joan Stevens' review of *Three* in the *Listener* suggested that Ashton-Warner's popularity was at a low point. The small accompanying photo showed the author looking particularly old and wrinkled, and the novel was recommended only to "Ashton-Warner fans" (1971, p. 71). With the publication of *I Passed This Way* and the presentation of the New Zealand Book Award in 1980, Stead was optimistic that Ashton-Warner's work would experience a "return to favour in New Zealand" (1981a, p. 58). Yet despite his optimism, nothing changed. The posthumous reissue of *I Passed This Way* in 1985 sparked only a brief, derogatory review in the *Listener*, condemning Ashton-Warner's ideas on education as "a measure of how far we've come" (Rountree & Williams, 1985, p. 64). Ashton-Warner's final publication, *Stories from the River*, earned her

Michael King's (1986) dismissive review and a concluding "Publish and be damned?" from *Landfall* (Bentley, 1987, p. 368). The situation baffled Stead, who wrote in the introduction to *Kin of Place*

> Then there was the contrary case of Sylvia Ashton-Warner, my advocacy producing no response at all, certainly no sign (or none apparent to me) of a revival of serious interest in her work—a fact all the more puzzling when considered against the background of 1980's feminism and the determined search in universities for neglected women writers. (2002, p. 4)

It remains to be seen whether Ashton-Warner's writing will experience the revival of interest that so many of our other neglected women writers have enjoyed in recent years. She is a significant New Zealand novelist whose work has come to exist at the very edges of our literary canon. Whether the novels themselves justify the criticism or neglect they have received is a matter open to reinvestigation.

Part Two: *Incense To Idols*: "Anyway, where is Tui these days with his tongue and his bird exhibitionism?"[2]

Landfall described *Incense to Idols* as a "resounding failure" (Day, 1961, p. 91). Joan Stevens called it "exasperating", referring to its "hysteria" and "muttered, turgid prose" (1961, pp. 107–8). Although the *Listener* reviewer did go against the grain, to say that "no page is tedious and the fabric of the writing is often brilliant", he too concluded firmly that, "[the] point of arrival is Erewhon" (Hall, 1960, p. 13).[3]

C. K. Stead proposed that "*Incense to Idols* was too much for her readers in New Zealand" and that "it was the […] wit and extravagance of it all that was found offensive" (1981a, p. 57). *Incense to Idols* was an expression of everything Ashton-Warner

---

2 Ashton-Warner, *Bell Call*, 1964, p. 231.
3 The Erewhon reference is to Samuel Butler's novel *Erewhon* which, based on his experiences in New Zealand, describes a fictional country that is not the utopia it first appears to be.

found lacking around her. It might be her own voice, rather than Hugh's, that exclaims, "I'm determined to have you glamorous and mysterious! I'm short of glamour and mystery" (*Incense to Idols*, 1960, p. 29).

The glamour of *Incense to Idols* was in radical contrast to the work of other New Zealand writers at the time. Indeed, New Zealand critics lacked the vocabulary to define what the novel was trying to do. Perhaps Ashton-Warner again speaks through Hugh when he asserts, "My own [sentences] would be far too original; you'd barely understand a word" (p. 50).

The story of a French concert pianist's relationships with various "playmates" and her increasing struggle with morality was never going to achieve great success here. The local critical mindset, characterised by heaviness and cynicism, ensured that *Incense to Idols* was bound to be misunderstood. A distaste for European decadence led to critics finding a flawed technique in the work. This was unfair, for the narrative is anything but "muttered, turgid prose". It is in fact tight, often sparkling, with sharply drawn, memorable characters. Its playfulness and comedy are perhaps its most misunderstood aspects. Beneath the dramatic religious themes, *Incense to Idols* also reveals a fascinating dialogue of a New Zealand writer's struggle to accept, and to be accepted by, her native country.

New Zealand context

The novel is grounded in a very concrete, small-town New Zealand setting, which various clues identify as Hastings. Like the "towering sheep-truck with double decks [that] thunders down the road, home from the sale-yards" (p. 247), the detailed descriptions of Hastings suggest an intimate familiarity. Like Germaine, Ashton-Warner may have worried that "I might bore you ... if I start preaching about ... the voices of bodgies and widgies at corners laughing and talking and whistling" (p. 56)—but more probably that she would bore herself. She seems to have confidence (perhaps misplaced) that if, like Germaine, she crashes into the clock towers of small-town New Zealand with her excesses, they "[could] take it; reinforced concrete" (p. 98).

Germaine certainly revels in these excesses. Rain at night becomes "the diamanted rain spangling street-length in the muted neon lights" (p. 127), and blossoms are transformed into "millions and millions of glamorous pink pearls" (p. 211). Yet it is Germaine herself who epitomises the glamour of this novel. "I'm mad on myself I'm so luscious" (p. 75), she confesses. It's easy to see why *Landfall* called the novel "a magazine-reader's fantasy of high fashion". She persistently describes her outfits in the language of advertising, describing one, for example, as "a two-piece dress in crease-resistant tweed with smart braid trimming. Lightweight and crisply textured for year-round fashion" (p. 13).

Interestingly, in Ashton-Warner's novels the characters themselves frequently pre-empt outside criticism. For example, a character accuses Germaine of being "concerned more with style than with meaning" (p. 114). Her critics however, within the text and outside it, overlook the real enjoyment of beauty and luxury that is expressed in her loving detailing of fabric: "Talbot's blend of eighty per cent wool and twenty per cent rabbit hair" (p. 26). In her quest to perfect the art of style, Germaine injects beauty into the very movements of life, resulting in a correspondingly luxurious language

> I am in the glorious indigo of the Chinese gown, luxury-loomed and fashion-fresh, a spectacular garment amounting to a way of life, making every movement spectacularly beautiful. (p. 19)

Germaine suggests that New Zealand society could benefit from her attitude towards beauty, as she complains, "why does everyone dress the same in New Zealand? All the women in skirts and cardigans and all the men in grey? Is it a national uniform?" (p. 18)

Germaine is also continually frustrated by the New Zealand male's clumsiness and his reticence to participate in the playful side of the erotic; they are "furtive, New Zealanders, about women, like some wicked secret" (p. 25). The novel defies the nation's staid morality by making the erotic of central importance. As Hugh succinctly admits, "eroticism is not easy to talk about with decorum, nevertheless it is the mainspring of creation" (p. 114). One intriguing aspect of Germaine's personality that directly contradicts Joan Stevens' verdict of "hysteria" is that Germaine—on the surface at least—is typically emotionless. Her response to an outburst by Leon is coldly antagonistic: "Monsieur, the course of your emotions is too conventional" (p. 58). Only the men of *Incense to Idols* become emotional; Germaine finds it embarrassing

> Can't you men be pathetic? Especially when you're in the heart's confessional. But I never was one for pathos. Didn't I say somewhere that souls were complicating? I meant to. If only we could close this embarrassing scene! (p. 63)

Emotions notwithstanding, Germaine's extravagance undeniably stands out both in the context of New Zealand literature and in the world of the novel. Characters find the "extraordinary virtuosity" (p. 241) of her piano playing bewildering and a little shocking. The culture Germaine finds herself in is one where congregations "[huddle] towards the back" (p. 10). Again and again in this novel there is sharp criticism of "the celebrated Common Level of this country where the efficient are denigrated and the inefficient bolstered" (p. 171). Germaine comes to realise that in New Zealand, "compliments are suspect. Admiration must be camouflaged by talk of the weather" (p. 96). And the Rev Guymer has a list of "twenty-three personal commandments" entitled "How to avoid slights from New Zealanders"

> Never be your real self with a New Zealander [...] Abandon sincerity; let no man see your inner self [...] Never speak with real seriousness to anyone. Never show your happiness or unhappiness [...] Never utter anything important to you [...]. (p. 175)

Doctor John comes to the conclusion that

> we New Zealanders, tucked comfortably away behind a Woollen Curtain, are likely to get like that, the ones who have not traveled. We either see the very worst in ourselves or the very best in ourselves and scream to high heaven about it. (p. 81)

Leon identifies Guymer as an artist existing in a country where "we penalise originality,/we crucify sensitivity,/we sentence our artists to ostracism and exile" (p. 234). There are obvious parallels between Guymer's experience and Ashton-Warner's own feelings as an artist. Take too, Germaine's frustrated outburst, employing an imaginative stream of insults: "You boorish Néo-Zélandais. You insular, wool-brained, mutton-fed, butter-spread, rugby-bred, beer-blind antipodean!" (p. 164). Doctor John counters her frustration with typical antipodean defensiveness: "Then why-the-devil-don't-you-get-out-of-here" (p. 164). However, both Guymer and Germaine's vehement accusations could be construed, as Leon recognises, as "the hatred of the rejected lover" (p. 180). Three pages after her outburst, Germaine admits that she is "falling for ... this funny little country", and finds herself "fascinated; by its orchards, the holiness of its sheep, the sanctity of its football and racing" (p. 167).

Indeed, running counter to the novel's overt critique are recurrent intimations of national pride. Guymer calls attention to New Zealand's "both marvelous and dreadful vitality", and acknowledges that it is "a country with this capacity ... for originality and drive" (p. 42). An acute analysis of "the spirit of New Zealand" is offered by Leon, who observes that "It is still *in utero* here. It only achieves birth abroad. It needs more air than can be found behind a Woollen Curtain" (p. 115). Despite this somewhat pessimistic evaluation, Leon also offers the most inspiring and slightly surprising insight into the New Zealand creative environment

> I'll tell you something that no one knows. New Zealand's national sport is not football; it's music. They don't know it, that's all. New

Zealanders can see all right but they're far too secretive to admit it. Besides ... it's the utter beauty of the place; the brilliant light, the purity of the colours. (p. 184)

Germaine too exclaims, "How bright this New Zealand sun!" (p. 18), and later in the novel wishes that "when I was born I had been dumped in a spring orchard in New Zealand rather than on a bellowing grand [piano] in Paris" (p. 238).

Ambivalence

Such comments reflect Ashton-Warner's own ambivalence about her country. Like Germaine, she is attracted to the physical realities of New Zealand. Luxury is, after all, something that can be touched, seen, heard and tasted. Germaine's conviction is that if she is ever touched by "soul", "it will be through the material and the mortal" (p. 76). She prefers "the wonderful world of the understandable and tangible: bitumen, metal, wood, stone, leaves, flowers and the jukebox down the street" (p. 49). Accordingly, she feels that New Zealand, "in spite of its import controls and income madness is the very place for people like me" (p. 167). Of the three trees on her property, Germaine prefers the tōtara, which is "rough and reasonable, his trunk firmly in the ground and wanting only what he can see for himself" (p. 36). She also approves of a beautiful tree, "whose name nobody knew, throwing back the sun from her bright foliage" (p. 36).

The beautiful tree clearly symbolises Germaine. Her true name is not known by many either, because she chooses to be known as the stereotypically ordinary "Mrs. Jones". She maintains that there is "Nothing to live up to in Mrs. Jones. No obligations, no glamour and no spurious mystery" (p. 98). But despite her insistence that she is 'just an ordinary girl" (p. 61), Germaine emits a strong sense of unreality. Again, the novel's characters pre-empt critical skepticism. Hugh accuses, "for all your talk of realities you don't quite ring authentic yourself" (p. 112).

This skepticism echoes the *Landfall* reviewer's lament: "If only we could [...] believe in her!" (Day, 1961, p. 91). But Ashton-Warner seems to embrace this sense of unreality. Germaine herself becomes increasingly unsure of her existence. She can be read as the artist struggling in New Zealand to be accepted for what she is, dealing with the subsequent isolation and self doubt. She reflects that

> I haven't really struck roots in this country, not deep enough anyway. Nothing is joined up as the rain joins everything together [...] You can laugh but ... what I feel is ... is that I'm something not attached. Something with no sources to draw on. (p. 134)

In the moments building to her suicide she has irretrievably lost a fixed sense of herself, asking, "Am I anyone at all?" (p. 280).

These are valid anxieties for any artist (a theme which will be picked up again in *Bell Call*), but particularly for one working in a conservative and often oppressive society. Add to this the clear preoccupation with what this country is—both its restrictions and its unique benefits, and *Incense to Idols*, rather than being written off and forgotten about, becomes instead rich material in the ongoing exploration of our national literature. *Incense to Idols* is a fascinating text precisely because of its difference to the strong regional emphasis of New Zealand literature. At the time of its publication, critics could not understand the insertion of flamboyance, exoticism, glamour and artistic indulgences into a small-town setting. The arrival of *Incense to Idols* on our literary scene is perhaps best described by Leon when he exclaims

> this dramatic appearance of a compatriot however young, however ... exotic ... your plunging from the sun into my shadows like this. Comprehension, my dear Madame, takes time. (*Incense to Idols*, 1960, p. 16)

Bell Call: "extraordinarily ordinary"[4]

After the exotic glamour and luxury of *Incense to Idols*, Ashton-Warner produced a novel that is extraordinarily ordinary. Set in a semirural New Zealand community, the action of *Bell Call* is centered around the local school but never explicitly within it, distinguishing the novel from *Spinster* while retaining the benefits of Ashton-Warner's familiarity with this environment. The action is grounded in the cyclical movements of the everyday: people coming and going, conversations, the daily (though removed) routine of school, the cycles of the seasons and school holidays. Beneath the apparent mundanities of *Bell Call*, however, is a world that it is infinitely more beautiful, varied, absurd and grotesquely comical than is generally recognised. Into this setting, Ashton-Warner places a writer, Dan, as her central character. Woven into the fabric of the ordinary then is an intimate exploration of what it is to write: the relationship of writing to daily life, the imagination and the frustrations of language.

It is difficult to define the sense of beauty that infuses every small, ordinary movement in this novel. It is beautiful because it evokes instant recognition: for example, when Dan makes the regular 50 km drive to his daughter Angela's farm "in the heart of the country at the foot of the high blue ranges" (*Bell Call*, 1964, p. 18), we hear the "tires crackling on the unpaved metal" (p. 137), and see "the mother plunging across the paddock like a shooting star to chase the turkeys from the garden" (p. 317). Although the novel delves into more adventurous themes like freedom and discipline, it remains grounded in these very ordinary images and moments.

However the community in *Bell Call* is more varied than its typical New Zealand regionalist representation. It includes writers, artists, lecturers and alternative thinkers, all of whom are aware of a greater global context. Many have been overseas: Dan has taught "all over

---

4   Ashton-Warner, *Incense to Idols*, 1960, p. 98.

Asia" (p. 109) and Tarl has already dragged her family "all round the world ... America, Britain, the Continent, back to New Zealand" (p. 93), and, as Dan suggests, could potentially take off to a number of obscure and exotic-sounding Asian locations: "Places like Isfahan, Zahidan, and ... a little place called Oomsbahn on a little island called Bahrain" (p. 104). They are cultured, appreciating good coffee and wine: Dan buys "coffee beans from Madagascar" (p. 297). And they habitually think about and discuss not only the ideas of great thinkers and writers—Goethe and Whitman are two—but their own ideas on topics like art, writing and freedom.

Bell Call also exposes ordinary New Zealand as absurd and grotesquely comical. Tarl and her brood are, Dan discovers, unorthodox visitors: "Over the fence they are always climbing with the barbed wire on top and the blackberry" (p. 111). Young Ben is revealed as having "four rows of bottom teeth" (p. 208). Even when absurdity escalates into grotesqueness and gore, plausibility remains solid. Bloody images in *Bell Call* result from everyday accidents and violence. For example, little Homer "runs a nail through his foot and [is carried] screaming and bleeding through the house, dripping into the kitchen" (p. 74).

Dan, the writer, perceives these images in terms of their sensational value and potential as source material, and thus experiences them with a kind of macabre enjoyment and gratitude. He has a writer's need to be up close to humanity in all its violence and bloodiness, acknowledging that "he wants to be close to the source of sensation, in the front row of the stalls where he always sits" (p. 110).

As a writer, Dan's perception of the world extends to seeing the people around him as characters. He remarks that "everyone's too convincing in this drama" (p. 131). His constant complaint is that he "can't avoid seeing everyone's damned side of a question" (p. 74). For Dan, it is an affliction that threatens to overwhelm his own identity

> It's this fatal inescapable identification of the artist with others. He becomes, he *is*, these people [...] You find a man like me living the lives of others ... a great sponge mopping up everything near him. I live their lives not *as though* they were my own, but *because* they are my own. Very very nice for art, of course. But for me as a man ... a man? Who, me? I'm not a man [...] I am nobody. I am everybody. I'm not I: I'm that fantail flirting out there. I'm Angela and Rod and the babies [...] Which is the reason I'm always on everyone's side, because each side is my own. It's why I die of conflict. (p. 218)

The writer is "a multiple soul" who must necessarily experience a "multiple response" (p. 131). This is distressing and exhausting for Dan, who laments, "I'm not geared to reality. Reality makes me sick. I belong to unreality, to the estates of the imagination" (p. 131).

Dan exists in two, equally legitimate, worlds: reality and the imagination. *Bell Call* explores the relationship between these two worlds and the shifting dominance of one over the other. For Dan, the imagination is a "drug that makes reality endurable" (p. 51). Such a powerful force becomes, for Dan, more real than "reality". When he is writing, "reality changes character; changes location", and, as his inner creations "expand and take on form, their bodies all but tangible", he feels that "others [are] the shadow, they the substance" (p. 72).

This can be an "ecstatic and dangerous reversal" (p. 31). Making "the difficult journey from the inner world out" (p. 73) is not easy, and interruptions—the intrusion of reality—can be disastrous. Tarl's constant interruptions, her "armfuls and armfuls of life" (p. 311), have a fatal effect on Dan's imaginary world. Dan finds to his frustration, that his inner creatures have "less light and life. [...] They no longer propel themselves, no longer live lives of their own" (p. 147). He finds himself "laboriously composing" (p. 147). Reality triumphs over the imagination, and in an inversion of Dan's hierarchy, Tarl asserts that "[w]ords are words and nothing else [...] Only the present is real"

(p. 56). Words can become, for the writer, a frustratingly inadequate medium to work with, and Dan takes the only course of action he sees possible to deal with "the entire neat stack [of pages] grown over a couple of years": he buries it in the compost (p. 228).

Bell Call, in its ordinariness (however extraordinary), avoids many of the problems that *Incense to Idols* encountered, with its unantipodean exoticism and overt criticism of New Zealand society—yet is one of our most under-read and underacknowledged novels. In *Bell Call*, Ashton-Warner displays an acute understanding of what it is to be a writer, including the writer's necessary and sometimes difficult relationship with reality. The writer needs the human drama that goes on around her, but equally needs solitude and space away from it—perhaps comparable to Ashton-Warner's own drama played out against her "native country" and her need to be the neglected genius. Though I lacked the space to explore it here, *Three* (1970) has suffered a fate much the same as *Bell Call*, in that it is as ignored as it is well written.

Conclusion

There are several possible explanations for Ashton-Warner's work as a writer becoming neglected. The focus on her work as an educator, and the preoccupation with a personality that polarised people, have played a significant part. But also, the author's immediate and ongoing international popularity and reputation was in conflict with a particularly vigorous nationalism. The perception of Ashton-Warner as an outsider was increased by her insistence on foreign protagonists and criticism of New Zealand's oppressive society. Critics misread an emotional hysteria in her work, predominantly in *Spinster* and *Incense to Idols*. Growing antagonism between Ashton-Warner and her native country was fuelled by personal frustrations with the author's inconsistencies and eccentricities.

Interest in Ashton-Warner's novels diminished as a result of the unfortunate progression of publication—*Spinster* overshadowed the succeeding novels, *Teacher* showed that she was a teacher rather than a writer, and *Incense to Idols* simply destroyed many people's interest. And finally, the representation of Māori in her writing, and in *Spinster* and *Greenstone* specifically, has been increasingly viewed as problematic.

But the novels of Sylvia Ashton-Warner should certainly not be relegated to the compost heap. They are novels that deserve to be read and enjoyed—but also investigated. They contain a wealth of material that could be drawn on for extremely interesting and creative academic work.

References

Ashton-Warner, S. (1958). *Spinster*. London: Secker & Warburg.

Ashton-Warner, S. (1960). *Incense to idols*. London: Secker & Warburg.

Ashton-Warner, S. (1963). *Teacher*. New York: Simon & Schuster.

Ashton-Warner, S. (1964). *Bell call*. New York: Simon & Schuster.

Ashton-Warner, S. (1966). *Greenstone*. New York: Simon & Schuster.

Ashton-Warner, S. (1967). *Myself*. New York: Simon & Schuster.

Ashton-Warner, S. (1970). *Three*. New York: Knopf.

Ashton-Warner, S. (1972). *Spearpoint: 'Teacher' in America*. New York: Knopf.

Ashton-Warner, S. (1980). *I passed this way*. Wellington: A.H. & A.W. Reed (First published in 1979, New York: Knopf).

Ashton-Warner, S. (1986). *Stories from the river*. Auckland: Hodder & Stoughton.

Author's 'Heaven'. (1998, 24–25 October). *New Zealand Herald Weekend Property*.

Bentley, J. H. (1987). [Review of *Stories from the River*]. *Landfall*, 41(3), 366–368.

Curnow, A. (1987). *Coal Flat* revisited. In Peter Simpson (Ed.), *Look back harder: Critical writings 1935–1984*. Auckland: Auckland University Press.

Day, P. (1961, March). [Review of *Incense to Idols*]. *Landfall, 15(1)*, 88–91.

Gibbons, P. (1991). Non-fiction. In Terry Sturm (Ed.), *The Oxford history of New Zealand literature in English*. Auckland: Oxford University Press.

Hall, D. (1958, 6 June). The tenderest art. *Listener, 38*, 12–13.

Hall, D. (1960, 23 December). On this high horse. *Listener, 43*, 12–13.

Hall, D. (1963, 29 November). Her native heath. *Listener, 49*, 18–19.

Hall, D. (1968, 2 February). Her own tradition. *Listener*, 21.

Hood, L. (1984, 2 June). Sylvia Ashton-Warner 1908–1984. *Listener, 107*, 24.

Hood, L. (1988). *Sylvia! The biography of Sylvia Ashton-Warner*. Auckland: Viking.

Jones, L. (1990). *Barbed wire and mirrors* (2nd ed.). Dunedin: Otago University Press.

Jones, L. (1991). The novel. In Terry Sturm (Ed.), *The Oxford history of New Zealand literature in English*. Auckland: Oxford University Press.

Jones, J. & Jones, J. (1983). *New Zealand fiction*. Boston: G. K. Hall.

King, M. (1986, June). The novel as social history. *Metro, 6*, 160–162.

McCormick, E. H. (1959). *New Zealand literature: A survey*. London: Oxford University Press.

McEldowney, D. (1969). Sylvia Ashton-Warner: A problem of grounding. *Landfall, 23(3)*, 230–245.

Munro, D. H. (1958). [Review of *Spinster*]. *Landfall, 12(3)*, 280–282.

Murray, S. (1998). *Never a soul at home: New Zealand literary nationalism in the 1930s*. Wellington: Victoria University Press.

Pearson, W. H. (1958). Attitudes to the Maori in some Pakeha fiction. *Journal of the Polynesian Society, 67(3)*, 211–238.

Rhodes, W. (1969). *New Zealand novels*. Wellington: New Zealand University Press.

Rountree, K., & Williams, M. (1985, 9 November). Artist and teacher [Review of *I Passed This Way*]. *Listener, 111,* 64.

Shallcrass, J. (1969, 17 January). Tolerance for change [Review of *Myself*]. *Listener, 60,* 16.

Shallcrass, J. (1980, 14 June). Teacher, writer. *Listener, 95,* 68.

Shallcrass, J. (1984). In memoriam Sylvia Ashton-Warner. *Landfall, 38*(3), 342–344.

Stead, C. K. (1981a). Sylvia Ashton-Warner: Living on the grand. In *In the glass case: Essays on New Zealand literature* (pp. 51–66). Auckland: Auckland University Press.

Stead, C. K. (1981b). Preliminary: From Wystan to Carlos—modern and modernism in recent New Zealand poetry. In *In the glass case: Essays on New Zealand literature* (pp. 139–159). Auckland: Auckland University Press.

Stead, C. K. (2002). Introduction. In *Kin of place: Essays on 20 New Zealand writers.* Auckland: Auckland University Press.

Stevens, J. (1961). *The New Zealand novel: 1860–1960.* Wellington: A. H and A. W Reed.

Stevens, J. (1971, 27 December). Taut Triangle. *Listener, 68,* 71.

Author

Emily Dobson read and investigated Sylvia Ashton-Warner during her honours year at Victoria University of Wellington. Following a master's degree in Creative Writing, she published a collection of poetry, *A Box of Bees*, in 2005, and travelled to Iowa University as the Glen Schaeffer Fellow. She lives in rural Hawkes Bay and is married to a beekeeper.

Email: disgruntledgoat81@yahoo.co.nz

CHAPTER 5

Were Sylvia Ashton-Warner's educational ideas really ignored In New Zealand?: The origins of *Teacher*

Geraldine McDonald

This chapter reports on New Zealand educationist Geraldine McDonald's forensic investigation into the first published versions of Sylvia's teaching scheme.

A call, posted on the Internet, for papers for a proposed book, described Sylvia Ashton-Warner as the subject of "silencing, exclusion, and book burning" (Robertson, 2002). In North America, and to some extent in New Zealand, it is believed that Sylvia could not get her educational theories published in New Zealand. *Teacher* was first published in 1963 and has been described as "a book that fell on completely closed ears in New Zealand" (Richards, 1970, p. 129). The main source for a belief in silencing, exclusion and closed ears appears to be Sylvia herself. In her "Letter to My American Editor" in *Teacher*, she answered some questions posed by Robert Gottlieb. She writes of a

> hoped-for publication of my work in my country by a New Zealander with passion and energy ... but it has failed like all the others (*Teacher*, 1986, p. 19)

> It is true that I have been trying to get this Creative Teaching Scheme published in my country for seven eventful years. I kept it here these seven years, trying, hoping, waiting, crippled with family loyalty. I stubbornly wanted it to come out in my own country in my own lifetime ... not after. (*Teacher*, 1986, p. 22)

In fact her teaching scheme had been published in New Zealand in the 1950s (Hood, 1988, 1990; Middleton, 2006) and a version was being printed in New Zealand which, by 1961, had reached the stage of being advertised, when Sylvia decided to withdraw it (Hood, 1988).

This chapter pieces together a background to this contradiction by tracing Sylvia's publishing identity, and the productive tension between her identity as a writer and as a teacher/educationist. Also squarely addressed here is the question of the originality of her educational ideas and practices.

Writer and theorist

During his sessions with Sylvia following her 1939 breakdown, Dr Donald Allen, a neurologist with a great interest in Freud, acknowledged her as a writer. Sylvia reported his advice in *I Passed This Way*, published in the United States in 1979 and in New Zealand in 1980. "You're a writer" he said (*I Passed This Way*, 1980, p. 282). No doubt Sylvia had earlier informed him that she was a writer and the information encountered no disbelief. His advice was offered in the interests of catharsis and healing but, in effect, it gave her permission to devote herself to writing (*I Passed This Way*, 1980, pp. 260–283). Her first prose work published as an adult, was a short story which appeared in the *New Zealand Listener* in 1948. The author's name was given as Sylvia Henderson.[1]

Sylvia writes of her great love of art, music and writing, but no great love of teaching. However, a metamorphosis appears to have occurred in the early 1950s when she "became" an educational theorist. By that time Sylvia held a psychoanalytic interpretation of the basis of behaviour. She developed a theory about the value of words which arose from the emotions of fear and sex lodged in a child's undermind. She saw a relationship between such words and the child's ability to remember and read them in preference to other words. On this basis she developed an introduction to reading which depended on the elicitation of these key words and their recording in writing. She refers to her years at Fernhill School (in the village of Ōmahu, near Hastings) as the time when she developed this theory. .

I think Sylvia's educational theory has to be seen in three segments. In the first the focus is on the language of beginning reading books for children whose first language is not standard English. In what she called her transitional readers, or Ihaka books, after the child who was their central character, Sylvia used the kind of language spoken by her young Māori pupils, and the stories were based on the

---

[1] Sylvia added Ashton to her original surname of Warner, and as an author used a range of names: Sylvia Henderson, Sylvia, S. Ashton-Warner and Sylvia Ashton Warner. In her work at Simon Fraser University she called herself Mary or Mere "who was five years old". The name Ashton was a family name. Sylvia's father's name was Francis Ashton Warner.

experiences of a child in a rural Māori settlement. For these books she was both author and illustrator. The second segment of her theory consists of the key vocabulary as the foundation of her reading and writing scheme, an approach which she referred to as "organic". For the third segment she developed a more comprehensive theory of teaching founded on creativity and its release.

Dates for the emergence of the complete scheme can be established. The Hendersons went to Fernhill School in 1949. A remark by Jack Richards (1970, p. 129), an expert in bilingualism who endorsed Sylvia's use of a the form of English used in a rural Māori village ("pā-vernacular"[2]), provides confirmation of this timing

> When I first wrote to Sylvia Ashton-Warner in 1968, she sent a telegram which began 'Congratulations on being the first New Zealand educationalist in the 18 years since its conception to approach me directly about my work'. (Richards, 1970, p. 132)

These dates confirm the early 1950s as the time of emergence of what Sylvia called her Creative Teaching Scheme.

What influences in the early 1950s converted someone who had long resisted being identified as a teacher into someone who spoke with authority on how to get Māori five-year-olds started on reading, how to run an infant classroom, how to teach maths and science, how to ignore a workbook and how to maintain classroom control? I think there were at least two key players. One was a school inspector and the other was an editor. I also suggest that a switch in Sylvia's notion of who she was occurred between the first publication, in 1952, of an article explaining the key vocabulary (Sylvia, 1952) and the subsequent publication, in 1955, of the same article, quite unchanged (Sylvia, 1955). The key vocabulary was first published in a journal which had no special interest in educational matters. It was republished in a journal devoted entirely to educational matters.

---

2   Pā originally referred to a fortified stronghold but today it is used to refer to a Māori village. A "pā–vernacular" is the form of English used in the village setting.

Publication of the teaching scheme

The initial explanation of Sylvia's educational ideas appeared in a journal called *Here and Now*. Robert Lowry, an Aucklander, was widely recognised for his work as a printer and typographer rather than as an editor, but in 1948 he and his wife Irene started what their daughter Vanya has referred to as "my parents' left-wing magazine" ("From the Wistaria bush", 2001), which, "for several years provided primarily a journal of opinion with some attention to the arts" ("Literature", 1966). *Here and Now* did not carry advice for teachers. However, the December 1952 issue included an article attributed to an author called "Sylvia", with the title "The key vocabulary". The key vocabulary was presented in autobiographical form, through the writer's report of her practices in an infant classroom and anecdotes about the Māori children in her class. It was clearly intended as a literary contribution. Embedded in the account was a description of a way of teaching reading based on a psychoanalytic theory of mind. But it was presented as a literary and not as an educational product. In 1955, the same article appeared in *National Education*, the journal of the primary teachers' organisation, the NZEI.[3] This time it was presented as an educational product.

National Education was a very different publication from *Here and Now*. Here it is described in the history of the NZEI by Ted Simmonds: By the 1930s, *National Education*

> was considered to be very valuable as a publicity vehicle in all senses of the term. It was regularly quoted by the press—not only for the 'political' comments, but also the articles on progressive educational developments which helped increase public understanding of the needs of children and the schools as seen by enlightened teachers. There was also a regular section providing practical suggestions for classroom teachers. (Simmonds, 1983, p. 127)

The early editors of *National Education* do not appear to have been professional journalists. They were probably teachers. But in October

---

3   The last issue of *Here and Now* appeared in November 1957.

1948, Russell Bond was appointed to the staff of NZEI, and his first issue of the journal appeared in November of that year. Bond had been educated at Canterbury University College. He had been a professional musician and had had 18 years of experience in daily journalism, including as a member of the literary staff on a daily newspaper ("New editor", 1948, p. 303). He wrote that in the 1950s, "I received from [Sylvia Ashton-Warner] a semi-coherent manuscript of jumbled text and drawings. This was my introduction to what was to become known as the key vocabulary in the context of organic teaching" (Bond, 1980, p. 115). Not only did he republish Sylvia's key vocabulary article from *Here and Now*, but he published further accounts by her over the course of a year. Therefore, it was Bond who first published Sylvia's fully realised version of her ideas on teaching and the curriculum. The outcome was her Creative Teaching Scheme. The articles are reprinted in this book (see Chapter 2).

Bond had arranged the first five articles as part of a series on the topic of "The Maori Infant Room". The first title was "Organic reading and the key vocabulary" (Sylvia, 1955). It has a short introduction that is an opinion piece, not autobiographical, and not in the *Here and Now* original. Sylvia refers to the problem of transition from one culture to another and then raises a topic which concerned her deeply and which she felt she had never managed to resolve, "the delay in the infant room". (She was referring to the practice of retaining Māori children in the junior classes for a year longer than was usual for non-Māori children.) This was followed by a section headed "* The key to vocabulary". (The "to" seems to have slipped in unnoticed.) Then there is an asterisked footnote (p. 392): "* This article is reprinted from the December 1952 issue of *Here and Now*".

"The Maori Infant Room" instalments are about literacy and the value of releasing destructive impulses in the interests of peace (Sylvia, 1955, 1956c, 1956d, 1956e, 1956f). They do not represent the whole of the Creative Teaching Scheme, but are a substantial part of it. Following the

Māori infant room set, three more instalments appear. They are about nature study and number (1956g), organic teaching (1956h) and "tone" (1956i). You will find this collection of eight articles in *Teacher*.

The first half of *Teacher*, the teaching scheme, includes the reproduction of the eight articles already edited, and in sensible order, more or less as published in *National Education* by Russell Bond. The account in *Teacher* starts with the fifth instalment from *National Education* (Sylvia, 1956f) and the final two instalments on the Māori infant room are transposed. There is a section inserted before the material on the Golden Section, on the transitional readers, which does not come from *National Education*. Some names have been changed. Photographs were included in the *National Education* articles but many more appear in *Teacher*. My favourite is one of a small boy dancing, which appears in "Organic Writing" (Sylvia, 1956d, p. 54) and in *Teacher* (Ashton-Warner, 1963/1986, p. 199). The most revealing alteration from the *National Education* account is on page 42 of *Teacher*. The article on Private Key Vocabularies in *National Education* (1956c) opens with the phrase "In my first article I said that", thus acknowledging a previously printed version. In *Teacher*, this passage has been altered to "I said earlier", referring to the text we are reading and thus disguising its origin.

Teacher even retained the original titles of the instalments and the new introduction to the key vocabulary in its *National Education* manifestation. There is no acknowledgement in *Teacher* or in any of Sylvia's other writing that the earliest article which contained material on the key vocabulary had been published in New Zealand in *Here and Now* in 1952.

A puzzle or two

Why did Sylvia Ashton-Warner decide to submit to a quite different journal something which had already appeared as a literary contribution? I once thought the most convincing explanation would be that Russell Bond had read her article in *Here and Now*, approached the author, asked for permission to reprint, and enquired whether she would expand her account to explain her theory of teaching. I have found absolutely no evidence that that was indeed the case.

However, while she was at Fernhill School, Sylvia's methods attracted the interest of Roland Lewis, the senior inspector in the district (see references to Mr Tremaine in *Teacher*, 1963/1986, p. 136 and following). Yes, she fell in love with him. Yes, she later turned against him. According to Hood, he suggested to Sylvia that she should develop a coherent account of her methods (Hood, 1988, p. 139) and he might well have suggested *National Education* as a suitable place to publish. Lewis also wrote her a note acknowledging something she had sent him in May 1953 (Hood, 1988, p. 152). He commented, "You must write a book some day." What kind of material might provoke that response? Since the *Here and Now* article "The key vocabulary" appeared the previous December it is very likely that she had sent him this. Lynley Hood said that Sylvia eventually submitted the account of her educational theory to both *National Education* and to Reed (the publishers). Russell Bond picked it up. He later wrote

> At that time I was impressed by the vitality that infused her writing, though less by the enthusiasm that overflowed in the arrangement of her text. I published one article immediately and four more later. This, I believe, was the first time the ideas of the key vocabulary appeared in print. If it was, *National Education* received no credit for it, either in *Teacher* which expounds the scheme, or in her latest book, *I Passed This Way*. (Bond, 1980, p. 115)

This is somewhat puzzling for more than one reason. The original piece on the key vocabulary as published in *National Education* in 1955 had stated quite clearly that it had already appeared in the journal *Here and Now*. Since Bond, as editor, had noted on the first page that the article had already been published, why did he claim first publication? It was, however, the first time the full Creative

Teaching Scheme appeared in print; an event which marked Sylvia's public emergence as an educational theorist and champion of organic teaching. On this broader definition Bond was indeed the first. No wonder he was irritated by the failure of *Teacher* and of Sylvia's autobiography *I Passed This Way* to recognise his contribution.

The second puzzle is that Bond says that he published five articles, but he actually published eight. Probably there was some confusion between the topic of introducing Māori children to reading and writing, and a broader teaching scheme covering education in general.[4] Bond's review of *I Passed This Way* appeared 25 years after the appearance of the key vocabulary and organic teaching in *National Education*. Lynley Hood commented on her meeting with Bond on 1 August 1984

> This morning I met Russell Bond, who published Sylvia's teaching scheme in *National Education* in the mid-fifties. He could not remember enough about it to answer my questions. (Hood, 1990, p. 89)

I strongly suspect that when he wrote his review in 1980, Bond's strength of feeling over the failure to acknowledge the role of his journal remained, but the details of the original publication had slipped from his memory.

Accompanying Bond's (1980) review of *I Passed This Way* is a reproduction of the opening page of the first article as published in *National Education*. But it is not a facsimile. It appears to be a proof in the process of being edited. Maybe Bond wanted to demonstrate that he had in fact edited it.

Only the first half of *Teacher* contains theoretical material. By and large the second half of *Teacher* is not theoretical. It consists of

---

4   In 1959, Sylvia offered a version of the Ihaka supplementary readers to NZEI for publication. Bond did not resign from the position of editor of *National Education* until 1959 (Simmonds, 1983, p. 227) and so was almost certainly involved in considering Sylvia's readers. They were turned down on the grounds of cost.

general scenes from the life of a school teacher in rural Māori schools in New Zealand. For example, it describes a sports competition, provides anecdotes about children and their families, and reproduces children's stories. On page 102, this anecdotal material is introduced as "from a diary". The first five pages are in fact a reprint of an article called "The least thing" from *Here and Now* (Sylvia, 1956a).[5] The final nine pages of *Teacher*, called "Remembering", are a reprint of "Floor", also published in *Here and Now* (Sylvia, 1956b).[6] Having traced the sources of this material, it is hard to avoid the conclusion that Russell Bond was the editor of most of the theoretical part of *Teacher*, and that Robert Lowry and *Here and Now* also deserve recognition.

I tried to find out whether any editorial correspondence from Bond's term as editor had been kept. Did he suggest that Sylvia might expand her account of reading and writing? Alas, there was nothing in the NZEI archives or in the Alexander Turnbull Library (Sharon Jones, personal communication, 27 May 2008).

There is yet another false lead to report. In the winter of 1947, Sylvia, in Waiomatatini, took time off from school, without permission, to attend concerts by the pianist Lili Kraus in Wellington and, no doubt, in the hope of meeting Walter Harris, whom she called "Pan". She describes being given a rough time by officers of the Department of Education when she tried to arrange a meeting with the Director of Education in Wellington, and so she went to get help from the NZEI, of which she was a member. The Secretary, Gordon Ashbridge, was overseas but she met the editor of *National Education*. The editor was given the task of talking to the officers of the department on her behalf. Sylvia had samples of her work which she said she would

---

5 A paragraph on controlling the class by commands from the piano has been omitted.
6 The original articles were all printed in a small font and in columns. In *Teacher* the columns become pages and are often generously illustrated. As a consequence "Organic reading is not new", for example, takes up one page in *National Education* and four-and-a-half pages in *Teacher*.

like to show Dr Beeby, the Director of Education, and so the editor must have seen what she had brought. My hopes were raised. Was this Russell Bond? Unfortunately, it was not. Russell Bond did not join NZEI until the following year.

The hidden truth

There were several small periodicals which flourished in the 1940s and 1950s and, following her story in the *Listener*, Sylvia continued to publish poems and short stories in periodicals such as *Numbers*, *NZ Monthly Review*, *Te Ao Hou* (an obituary), *Parent and Child*, and *Comment*, but I have been unable to find any more of her work in *National Education*.

Does an article cease to be literary if printed in *National Education*? In a list of Sylvia's literary publications compiled by The University of Auckland library (The University of Auckland, n.d.), the *Here and Now* article on the key vocabulary is present. But the identical article in *National Education* and the other instalments in that journal are not included. The account of the key vocabulary was first published as a literary impression and only later republished as part of a guide to teaching Māori children. A failure to treat publications in *National Education* as literature meant that the eight articles, which constituted Sylvia's Creative Teaching Scheme, were likely to be omitted from records of her publications.

It is very hard to shift beliefs once people are committed to them. Would it have been easier to discover that Sylvia's ideas had *not* been denied publication in New Zealand had *National Education* been readily accessible to the compilers of her writings? Would the truth have emerged if the crucial eight articles from *National Education* and three from *Here and Now* had been compared with their counterparts in *Teacher* (for discussion of this point see Gottlieb, Chapter 6, this volume)? And would Sylvia's statements in her "Letter to My American Editor" have been believed had *Teacher* included permission to reprint the material from *National Education* and acknowledged poor old Russell Bond and his struggles with a "semi-coherent manuscript"? After all, Bond was alive when *Teacher* was being prepared and could easily have been traced. In exploring Sylvia's publishing history I ended up with a strong sense of the injustice meted out to Russell Bond and *National Education*.

Sylvia's place as educational theorist

Although Sylvia's ideas were theoretical, they were presented in her writing, and later in her demonstrations to adults, as descriptions of her actual practices. That is, they were autobiographical; hence brief evaluations of her work as an educationalist have often been left to literary commentators. Her ideas have been subjected to surprisingly little critique from an educational viewpoint and very little empirical study in New Zealand. However, Sue Middleton (2006) has made a major study of the cultural origins of her ideas about teaching; Alison Jones (2006) has critiqued the key words that Sylvia collected; Geraldine McDonald, Helen Goldblatt and Marilyn Barlow (2003) compared the lives of Susan Isaacs and Sylvia Ashton-Warner and the reception of their respective ideas in New Zealand; and Marilyn Barlow (2007) has put the method of key words to the test in a classroom.

Were Sylvia's ideas original?

Although Sylvia possessed an amazing ability to convey in writing the emotional atmosphere of her creative classrooms, her actual practices were very similar to those reported by other New Zealanders who taught infants (Middleton & May, 1997). This meant that many New Zealand teachers recognised her methods as similar to their own. The key vocabulary, for example, was like "interest words" elicited by many teachers when children wrote their own stories.

The work of John Dewey, activity methods and progressive education were known to many New Zealand teachers. This is not to say that all were touched by the urge to be creative. In 2008, when New Zealander Brian Sutton-Smith, well known for his promotion of play, visited from the United States, he was asked about his earlier teaching career in New Zealand. He said that creativity was stomped on. In the 1940s, on Friday afternoons he played the children a piece of Beethoven and they had to invent stories to match. One day the principal came into the room and put a stop to it (Kitchin, 2008). But I suspect that Sutton-Smith was not teaching five-year-olds. The degree of freedom allowed in New Zealand schools has generally depended on the level of the class—the younger the children the greater the freedom.

Sylvia's claims have provoked responses from others. Gwendolen Somerset, who became a leader in the field of early childhood education and wrote on child development in psychoanalytic terms, was the sister of Joy Alley, whom Sylvia referred to as "Opal" in *I Passed This Way*. Gwen visited Pipiriki when both Joy and Sylvia were there. When she wrote her personal story, Gwen had obviously read *I Passed This Way*, and her own autobiography, *Sunshine and Shadow* (Somerset, 1988), was in part a challenge to Sylvia as an educational pioneer. As teachers of infant classes, both Sylvia and Gwen included dancing in their programmes; Sylvia following Isadora Duncan, and Gwen, English country dances. Sylvia played the piano, Gwen used the gramophone. Neither valued workbooks. Gwen, like Sylvia, wrote supplementary readers, but for older children. Both produced dramatic performances. Gwen painted backdrops. Sylvia drew murals. An important difference was that Gwen had been an infant mistress in the 1920s, not the 1940s.

According to her sister, Keri Kaa, the writer Arapera Blank admired Sylvia Ashton-Warner (personal communication, 21 October 2008). Arapera and Sylvia show a similar concern for the difficult relationship between a home culture and a different school culture, and both used stories to bring the experience of schooling to life. When she was invited by the editors of *The Maori People in the Nineteen-sixties* to contribute a chapter on the topic of intercultural stress, Blank responded with a touching short story, "One, two, three, four, five" (Blank, 1968).[7] In her story, a small Māori boy, Whaimata, recounts his first day at a school that appears to be populated by Māori children much like the schools in which Sylvia taught. The author describes how his family prepare him for school, and how the other children treat him once he gets there. He fears that there is a ghost in the boys' lavatory. The story includes a description of a creative classroom, a sympathetic teacher who played the piano, and, in a postscript, deals with the effect of schooling on Māori culture.

Sylvia's teaching methods are in the same intellectual mould as those promoted by Susan Isaacs, who directed the Malting House School in England in the 1920s, and who visited New Zealand as a speaker at a New Education Fellowship conference in 1937. Isaacs published two books based on careful observation of what the children did and said. Her first work was on intellectual development (Isaacs, 1930) and the second on social development (Isaacs, 1933). She then wrote a text called *The Children We Teach*, first published in 1932. The 12th edition appeared in 1954. This work was widely used in New Zealand teachers' colleges. Isaacs' ideas influenced teaching practice in both the United Kingdom and New Zealand. Sylvia lists the authors she has read (*I Passed This Way*, p. 354), but Susan Isaacs is not amongst them (see Middleton, Chapter 3, this volume).

Although orthodox psychoanalytic theory referred to love and hate rather than fear and sex as the main building blocks of the emotional basis of behaviour, Sylvia's descriptions of the "undermind" of a child were in keeping with the spirit of her times. In 1956 the lectures of the Wellington-based Association for the Study of Childhood

---

7 In a book of readings on Māori education, John Ewing and Jack Shallcrass reprinted Arapera Blank's "One, Two, Three, Four, Five" followed by an excerpt from *Spinster* by Sylvia Ashton-Warner.

were on the topic of psychoanalysis and childhood (Association for the Study of Childhood, 1957). Psychoanalysis informed what was taught to mothers in the Playcentre movement, where free play was being promoted as children's work. Self-expression was described as cathartic, a way of releasing emotions which might otherwise be destructive to the emerging self.

Conclusion

It seems clear that innovative and creative work was happening (and often with official encouragement) in New Zealand primary-school classrooms during the period Sylvia wrote about teaching. Sylvia's accounts of her ideas about teaching and descriptions of her classrooms remain lively and inspirational but, contrary to her claims that no one in New Zealand would publish her teaching scheme, it turns out that almost all the theoretical material, at least some of the diary entries, and many of the illustrations in *Teacher* can be traced to earlier publication in New Zealand. Two people appear to have had key roles in the gestation of Sylvia's teaching scheme. At Fernhill she received confirmation of her teaching practices from Roland Lewis, the senior inspector in the district, and through him, from others including academics. An article published originally as "autobiographical literature" was subsequently accepted by Russell Bond, the editor of an education journal to become part of her Creative Teaching Scheme. Both men influenced Sylvia's metamorphosis from reluctant teacher to education theorist.

References

Ashton-Warner, S. (1963/1986). *Teacher*. New York: Simon & Schuster.

Ashton-Warner, S. (1980). *I passed this way*. Wellington: A. H. & A. W. Reed.

Association for the Study of Childhood (1957). *Psychoanalysis and the study of personality: The 1956 lectures*. Wellington: Author.

Barlow, G. M. (2007). *Sylvia Ashton-Warner and children's words: A modern investigation*. Unpublished master's thesis, Victoria University of Wellington.

Blank, A. (1968). One, two, three, four, five. In Erik Schwimmer (Ed.), *The Maori people in the nineteen-sixties* (pp. 85–96). Auckland: Longman Paul.

Bond, R. (1980, 1 July). Who is Sylvia, what is she? *National Education*, 115.

From the Wistaria bush [promotional material]. (2001). Retrieved 29 January 2009 from http://web.auckland.ac.nz/uoa/aup/book/from-the-wistaria-bush.cfm

Hood, L. (1988). *Sylvia! The biography of Sylvia Ashton-Warner*. Wellington: Viking.

Hood, L. (1990). *Who is Sylvia?: The diary of a biography*. Dunedin: John McIndoe.

Isaacs, S. (1930). *Intellectual growth in young children*. London: Routledge & Kegan Paul.

Isaacs, S. (1932). *The children we teach: seven to eleven years*. London: University of London Press.

Isaacs, S. (1933). *Social development in young children: A study of beginnings*. London: Routledge.

Jones, A. (2006). Sex, fear and pedagogy: Sylvia-Ashton Warner's infant room. In J. Robertson & C. McConaghy (Eds.), *Provocations: Sylvia Ashton-Warner and excitability in education* (pp. 15–32). New York: Peter Lang.

Kitchin, P. (2008, 19 April). The importance of being playful. *The Dominion Post*, p. E10.

Literature—Literary periodicals and criticisn. (1966). In A. H. McLintock (Ed.), *An encyclopedia of New Zealand*. Retrieved 29 January 2009, from http://www.TeAra.govt.nz/1966/L/LiteratureLiteraryPeriodicalsAndCriticism/en

McDonald, G., Goldblatt, H., & Barlow, M. (2003). Susan and Sylvia: The fate of educational ideas. *New Zealand Journal of Educational Studies*, 38(1), 49–58.

Middleton, S. (2006). "I my own professor": Ashton-Warner as New Zealand educational theorist, 1940–1960. In J. Robertson & C. McConaghy (Eds.), *Provocations: Sylvia Ashton-Warner and excitability in education* (pp. 41–73). New York: Peter Lang.

Middleton, S., & May, H. (1997). *Teachers talk teaching 1915–1995: Early childhood, schools and teachers' colleges*. Palmerston North: Dunmore Press.

New editor of *National Education*. (1948, 1 November). 303.

Richards, J. (1970). The language factor in Maori schooling. In J. L. Ewing & J. Shallcrass, *An introduction to Maori Education: Selected readings* (pp. 122–132). Wellington: New Zealand University Press & Price Milburn.

Robertson, J. (2002, 18 March). CFP: Sylvia Ashton-Warner and excitability in education (5/1/02; collection). Message posted to Literary Calls for Papers Mailing List, archived at http://www.english.upenn.edu/CFP/archive/2002-03/0109.html

Simmonds, E. J. (1983). *NZEI 100: An account of the New Zealand Educational Institute: 1883–1983*. Wellington: New Zealand Educational Institute.

Somerset, G. L. (1988). *Sunshine and shadow*. Auckland: New Zealand Playcentre Federation.

Sylvia. (1952, December). The key vocabulary. *Here and Now*, pp. 26–28.

Sylvia. (1955, 1 December). No. 1: Organic reading and the key vocabulary. *National Education, 406*, 392–393.

Sylvia. (1956a, April). The least thing. *Here and Now*, pp. 23–24.

Sylvia. (1956b, June). Floor. *Here and Now*, pp. 25–27.

Sylvia. (1956c, 1 February). No. 2: Private key vocabularies. *National Education, 407*, 10–12.

Sylvia. (1956d, 1 March). No. 3: Organic writing. *National Education, 408*, 54–55.

Sylvia. (1956e, 3 April). No. 4: Organic reading. *National Education, 409*, 97–98.

Sylvia (1956f, 1 May). Organic reading is not new. *National Education, 410*, 141.

Sylvia (1956g, 1 August). Nature study and number: The Golden Section. *National Education, 413*, 248–251.

Sylvia (1956h, 3 September). Organic teaching: The unlived life. *National Education, 414*, 294–295.

Sylvia (1956i, 1 October). Tone. *National Education, 415*, 342–343.

The University of Auckland Library (n.d.). *Sylvia Ashton-Warner, New Zealand Literature File*. Retrieved 2 July 2008 from http://www.library.auckland.ac.nz/subjects/nzp/nzlit2/ashton.htm

Acknowledgements

I would like to thank Sharon Jones for information about Russell Bond, and Hugh Price for access to copies of *Here and Now*.

Author

Geraldine McDonald, PhD (Victoria University of Wellington), trained as a teacher. She worked for the New Zealand Council for Educational Research establishing an early childhood unit and then becoming its Assistant Director. A senior Fulbright Award took her to Teachers' College Columbia University. She has taught at Victoria University of Wellington and has a particular interest in women theorists, writing, with two colleagues, a comparison of the influence of Sylvia Ashton-Warner with that of Susan Isaacs.
Email: geraldine.mcdonald@clear.net.nz

CHAPTER 6

Publishing Sylvia: C. K. Stead talks to Robert Gottlieb

Robert Gottlieb

Robert Gottlieb was Sylvia Ashton-Warner's American editor and publisher. As a young editor in New York, Gottlieb published *Spinster* in 1958, and later Teacher (1963)—which Sylvia dedicated to him. Gottlieb also published *Incense to Idols* (1960), *Bell Call* (1965), *Greenstone* (1966), *Myself* (1966), *Three* (1970), Spearpoint (1972) and Sylvia's autobiography *I Passed This Way* (1979). New Zealand novelist C. K. Stead interviewed Robert Gottlieb by video link from New York before an audience at the International Sylvia Ashton-Warner Centennial Conference at The University of Auckland, New Zealand, on 10 August 2008.

C. K. STEAD: I thought I'd begin with a general approach to the subject of your role as Sylvia's editor. In fact we had one very interesting paper yesterday by Dr Judith Giblin James (James, 2008) who has read some of your correspondence with Sylvia, and she had also read an interview with you in *The Paris Review*. She had extracted some editing principles that were clearly yours and she advanced the interesting idea that since you were very young and you were Sylvia's editor very early in your career, you may in fact have formulated some of these principles in editing her work. And she gave examples of them. One was that a book can be improved simply by changing the title—which is a narrower form of the fact that you thought the central part of the editing process, the most important part, was the work on the beginning and the ending of a book. Another was that editing is just the application of the common sense of any good reader—and I thought the crucial word there was "good", not the common sense of any reader, but any good reader, and that an editor should save writers from themselves. First of all, do you recognise these principles; and can you tell us something about how you applied them in editing Sylvia; and maybe did you extract some of those principles from that early experience?

ROBERT GOTTLIEB: Well, you have to remember this all was 50 years ago. I first encountered Sylvia in 1958 and a lot of water has passed under my dam since then. At that point in my life I didn't have any principles. In fact I never had any principles until the interviewer from *The Paris Review* asked me for principles. I'm not an abstract kind of person. I just react and respond and say what I think. Not just in editing, but in life. I don't formulate. So anything I said to this very bright woman who interviewed me was what she forced me to think about. With Sylvia, the first book that we did together was *Spinster*. That book was already edited and published in England before I ever saw it. It was not an easy book to sell in America. I don't have the correspondence in front of me so I can't tell you for instance what I said about *Spinster* or *Three*, but I can tell you about Sylvia and me and how we worked and how we came together and in one particular case, which is *Teacher*, I can say a great deal because I essentially made that book, created that book.

I think everybody wants to hear what's of interest to you and what you remember most vividly and clearly.

Okay, let me give you the background. I was essentially a kid, although I didn't think I was. I first must have read *Spinster* before I was 27. I had published a wonderful novel, Sybille Bedford's *A Legacy*, which was very, very successful, and I was looking for another book of that quality that I could respond to very personally because publishing is just making public your enthusiasm—so you have to have the enthusiasm before you can do it well. One day I was having lunch with a literary agent named Monica McCall. I didn't know her very well. We had been thrown together in a highly tense and emotional situation involving a Broadway play and a writer who was insane, and a producer who was insane. I remember it was lunch at the Plaza Hotel so our meeting was already very glamorised and I adored her on sight and she me. So we were talking, talking, talking and she said to me "Would you by any chance be interested in a novel about a school teacher in New Zealand?" And I was about to say "you've got to be kidding", because why would I be interested in publishing a novel about a school teacher in New Zealand, when I remembered that I had already figured out that it wasn't the subject of the book that was important, it was how it was written and what it had to say. And I said "Sure, I'd love to read it."

She sent me the next day a finished copy of the hideous English edition of *Spinster*, which I read overnight. I called her in the morning and I said "This is absolutely wonderful and I would love to publish it." My colleagues and I worked very, very hard to bring it to the attention of book reviewers and book review editors, because again I was then working at Simon and Schuster, which was known as a commercial rather than a literary publishing house. Although they published a number of literary books, it was essentially commercial and they were not likely to think that a novel about New Zealand from Simon and Schuster was something they had to pay attention to. But somehow we captured the attention of the critical apparatus in America at that time. It got wonderful reviews and it actually crept on to the bottom of the *New York Times* bestseller list, which was a highly unlikely thing to have happen.

Meanwhile Sylvia and I were in correspondence and it was a very heightened correspondence. I was susceptible to the charm and intelligence of her writing and she clearly needed a lifeline to the outer world because she didn't have any. You know, the English publisher and she had no relationship and even with Monica McCall, her purported agent, they had never really had anything to do with each other. Monica got this book because she was representing the English publisher. But I was the first person, I think, in the outside world who connected with her and responded to her, and so she invested a great deal in this correspondence. I did too, because from her writing, from her letters, I loved her and was fascinated by her. So this correspondence quickly became quite personal.

In all her letters to me, up at the top where you would have the date and whatever town she was living in, they all started "From behind the Woollen Curtain". That was essentially the way she saw her life. It was clear to me that she felt trapped behind the Woollen Curtain, and frustrated. However, the fact that her book was being published in the outside world when she felt, as you know, that New Zealand had no use for her, was a tremendous boost for her psyche and for her ego—whatever you want to call those things. It was wonderful because suddenly she was internationally, if not nationally, known. I don't mean on a vast scale, but it was real, and as you know *Spinster* was chosen by *Time* magazine as one of the 10 best novels of the year. That was extraordinary.

By then she was writing *Incense to Idols*, and that's when we first started having an editorial correspondence. She was very, very available to the editing process. I mean very rarely did she take exception to things I suggested because the things I suggested were sane. She on this level was totally sane. The only problem we had was about the embryo and the wine glass, because as I remember it, this was an embryo when it was aborted, a couple of months old. But she had it in her book as this perfectly formed little person in the wine glass and I remember pointing out to her that as far as I knew, anatomy in New Zealand was the same as it was in the rest of the world. Babies at that age were like a little ... toenail of a shrimp. They were not little replicas of you and me. So then she wrote me back with a wonderful little drawing of a martini glass which would have a tiny little baby in it. Commonsense finally prevailed, although she did stick at it. But maybe she asked a doctor she knew.

I don't know whether you remember, but she did. She wrote you a comic letter, a funny letter, clearly not to be taken seriously, in which she said that foetuses behind the Woollen Curtain clearly advanced much more quickly than in New York ...

Exactly ...

... which was putting your image of the metropolis and the provinces in reverse. In fact we're much more advanced ...

That was not a real issue, it was just funny. That's my real memory of *Incense to Idols*. The book did well, but not as well as *Spinster*. It was a more difficult subject. One of the things that can make a book, as we say, "work" is if it reveals a new world to a readership, but not every great book does that. There are great books made up of common matters everyone is aware of. But when you come to a new world, some place that nobody knows anything about, the exotic aspect can really help launch a book, because it gives reviewers something to write about. You know, what do you write about novels? This is somebody's 11th novel and it's a little bit better or a little worse than the last one.

But if suddenly you're in a world of Māori school children and a beleaguered teacher who is coming up with the theory and it's very emotional and there's a love interest, and it's New Zealand … there's a subject that reviewers can get their teeth into! So that was very helpful. [I think people like books that give them] an entrée to a new world. *Spinster* did that for a number of people, including me. I was partly drawn to it because—what this was all about? I didn't know. I knew there were Maoris. I didn't know anything more than that they were an indigenous people in New Zealand.

When we got to *Teacher*, this was a completely different experience, one unlike any I have ever had—and by this time I had probably edited over 1,000 books. She wrote to me and said out of the blue, "I'm sending you all of my papers, diaries, letters, etc. about my teaching experience. They're all in boxes and there are cutouts from magazines and there are things that the children in school did and I can't live with them anymore and I've got to get them out of my garage and they've got to go somewhere, do something, make a book or throw them out, I don't care." So they arrived in my apartment in New York, several boxes filled with not disorganised material, but utterly unorganised material. She had just taken everything and flung it into cartons and posted it off. I had a long, narrow living room at that time. It's all completely visual memory: a long, narrow living room that, for some reason I don't recall, pretentiousness no doubt, was painted a kind of dark blue enamel. So I took all this material and I just put it in piles on the floor, which my then-wife wasn't too happy about. But nevertheless I prevailed and slowly over a period of about six months I sorted it and tried to figure out what the hell I had. Now you have to understand that a great deal of that material was duplicated. But it wasn't duplicated word for word. You know we didn't have xerox, we didn't even have copying machines. She certainly didn't. Everything was typed with carbons and there would be … I would find three pages, pages 8, 9 and 10, on a particular coloured paper. There didn't seem to be anywhere in this mass of material a 1 through 7 or 11 through 45. They were just three isolated pages and they seemed to be the same material that was in a whole other piece of material that was pages 36 through 45. But they were all different. Clearly she worried at this material and went over and over and over it, but she threw nothing out. Then there were the photographs. You all know the photographs that appeared in *Teacher*. A lot of them were coiled up, splotched negatives, others were splotched snapshots. They weren't in very good condition because I don't think the garage was air-conditioned. It had been hibernating there, so it was one great big mess. But the more I penetrated it and read, the more I thought it was wonderful. It was wonderful, wonderful material. So I started doing what you do.

It was like a giant jigsaw puzzle, except that with a jigsaw puzzle you know there is a real picture you're supposed to be achieving. Here there was no real anything. It was just what we made of it and I couldn't let anybody else work on it because it was too complicated and had to be in one person's head. Anyway, very slowly I figured out the structure of this book and sewed it all together. I chose the pictures and worked very closely with a designer I trusted and with a jacket designer I was very close to. The jacket, by the way, was based on the dust jacket for *Born Free*. That was the look I wanted because it incorporated block type colour and small photographs. She had said "Don't show it to me, I don't want to know, I may never even look at the finished book." I knew that was ridiculous and I said "I need a short introduction from you or foreword, so I'll send you the galleys." Of course she had things to say about what I had done but they were very modest and totally reasonable. And she did write something.

So we put this book out. And by an extraordinary piece of luck—I didn't quite know what this meant back then—it was reviewed on the front page of *The New York Times Sunday Book Review*, which was the number one launching pad for a major book. Anything reviewed on the front page of *The New York Times Book Review* was an immediate signal to all of *New York Times* readers and to the whole community this was something you had to pay attention to. A very sympathetic person who had been involved with poetry for children was given this book to review and just said "This is the greatest thing ever, this is a revelation, this is an astonishment, the world has to sit up and pay attention!" So the world did, because it had been told to by *The New York Times*.

So this book had an immediate success, not so much that it sold millions of copies, but that [it appealed to educators] across America—remember this was at a new period, a kind of revolutionary period, in America, the late '60s and '70s when everything was supposed to be new and untraditional. You were no longer allowed to learn reading by the way things sounded; you had to learn combinations of letters. It was completely hopeless; nobody could learn it. Educators were waiting for something new, and they found it in this book and this book was picked up by experimental educators all over America. It was a great thing to have happen. Of course, her theory when applied sometimes worked and sometimes didn't work, because you can have wonderful ideas but unless you're brilliant at deploying them, it's not going to work in the same way. This would be true of almost anything, anything about which you can develop theories. I'm sure Sylvia was a genius of a teacher, and when she then came up with her theories, she was a genius at applying them. I'm not sure that you or I could apply them to equal effect. That made no difference to all the people who thought they'd found the Holy Grail. So they all started to apply Sylvia's ideas, and then when Sylvia finally came to America and she started to apply them ... I wouldn't say people were disillusioned, I think by then people were wary; they understood that they couldn't be her. Who could be her? Who would want to be her?

So that is the story of *Teacher* as I remember it. It was thrilling for me because it was so interesting. The material was so interesting and doing it was so interesting. You know, I'm a puzzle solver. And it was a unique experience in my life and then it was a success too and it made her very happy.

When *Teacher* appeared there was this image of a book that had been rejected in New Zealand, that Sylvia wanted this book published, she wanted her theory published and revealed in New Zealand, but she hadn't been able to achieve this. And then it was published in New York, and part of the success of the book was not only that it was excellent in itself but that it was the book of a prophet who'd been rejected in her own country.

When Lynley Hood's biography [1988, pp. 170–172] of Sylvia appeared, we had a new story: that a book (to be called *Organic Teaching*) was submitted to a publisher called Bill Moore of William Heinemann Ltd in New Zealand. He spent a great deal of time on it, and with Sylvia, going backwards and forwards between Wellington and wherever she was—and working with typesetters—and then at the last minute, when he wanted her to sign a contract, she said "Go away, I've got a publisher in New York." When you read this in Lynley's book there's a disparity between the book that's about to be published in New Zealand and the story which you've just told about these boxes of material that went to New York being spread over the floor for months and gradually assembled into a book. Clearly there are two truths here. In reality they can't be irreconcilable, but they're not easy to reconcile.

And we know from Geraldine McDonald another story, another element, which is that everything that occurs in the first half of *Teacher*, with a few exceptions appeared in sequence in a periodical called *National Education* in New Zealand.

Well, that's certainly possible. Remember a lot of what I got was tear sheets of pieces, articles, reproductions of articles, and there was nothing that was a manuscript, but there was material from all kinds of places. Now for all I know Sylvia had shown a lot of material, offered a lot of material, to a publisher in New Zealand. That could very well be. I can't believe it was organised in a full manuscript because she would have sent me that. There was nothing organised in what I saw. What I saw was scraps, some of them had been published in I assume the kind of magazine you're talking about. I don't really remember what those pieces of paper were but they were not in an order. There was nothing that was coherent in terms of the structure of the book. Everything was coherent in itself and she could easily have shown that material to who knows who, I don't. I don't know about New Zealand educational publishing.

Everybody acknowledges your great role with Sylvia ...

I don't want my role acknowledged ... I'm just trying to get to the reality of the matter.

Well, it is acknowledged whether you want it or not. I'm an academic, but I'm also a fiction writer, and I really prefer this story according to a fiction writer to the story according to the academic researcher. I prefer the simple story. But it seems to me my role at this moment is to get somewhere in between.

I can offer nothing but what I experienced. Certainly she never told me that she had been or was in discussion with a New Zealand publisher. "I can't deal with this anymore," she said, "so you have to deal with it." Why I assumed that because she couldn't deal with it I had to deal with it, I don't quite know. She had that effect on me.

The other thing, before we move on to your late work with her, is that you said you were the first person she had connection with outside ...

As far as I know.

There she was behind the Woollen Curtain and it's certainly true, Lynley Hood makes a point that there were only two people with whom she had a long ongoing and important correspondence,

you and her son Elliot. All other correspondence is somewhat fragmentary and that in itself indicates how important the relationship was. But it's also true with Sylvia that everybody she had anything to do with was made to feel they were the only one, and without them she was just isolated, neglected. She had a tremendous talent for making people feel she needed them and life would be impossible without them.

Also she romanticised, because she was a romanticist if not, to put it politely, a fabulist. She needed to believe in ... look, at that time I wasn't thinking about what this correspondence was or what this relationship was. I was writing letters and she was writing letters. I didn't know anybody 40 years later would be interested and I'm still not sure why. She wrote me, I wrote her, it was very interesting, very touching often, and I felt I was giving her something I guess that she needed. And she must have been giving something I needed. It certainly wasn't for professional reasons. I had vast professional relationships. Part of it was the distance. If she were a writer in America or England where I went every year, I would have known her very well. We would have seen each other all the time, we would have had lunches, she would have come to my house for dinner, there would have been intercourse. Here there was nothing but a lifeline of correspondence, so we were abstract for each other. I discovered that when I read the manuscript of *I Passed This Way*, her autobiography. The most work I did on that book was to cut out probably 50 per cent or more of what she wrote about me, almost all of which was fantasy. She had created a "me" and that's what she thought I was. We all do that to a certain extent, but not on paper. A number of times I had to edit books in which I appeared and it's always hilarious. But this was over the top, and she had made inferences etc., etc. that just ... So I said "No, no, no, no, you've got it all wrong. I don't care what you say about your husband, about your children, about your country, about your teaching, but you can't tell these fantasies about me, because they're just not true." None of it was derogatory; it just wasn't true. So I dug my heels in there. So I was an invention in her head, and she being a novelist, I was a character in her novel. I am not a novelist. I have no creative impulse and I'm not a romantic nor a fabulist. So for me she was a wonderful writer who lived in New Zealand whom I was in close touch with.

A lot of the other parts of the book must be fable as well but ...

She was more in touch with the rest of her life than she was with me. I was an invention and I fed that invention because I wrote to her very directly and somewhat intimately, so she had material there and she used it to the best possible advantage, but not mine.

There was a period, particularly when she was in Vancouver when it seemed she was unwell and she was writing below her best. You were always very frank and diplomatic but honest with her. There were two books in particular which weren't published. One was called Barren Radiance **and one was called** Tenth Heaven. **Apparently she asked did you think that** Barren Radiance **was suggesting that the basic relationship was lesbian. You said yes. And this terribly stirred her and she abandoned the book. The only reference I've been able to find to** Tenth Heaven **is that it was her favourite. Do you remember anything about those at all?**

I wish I did, but I don't. Tenth Heaven—and this is just a wild guess—could part of that have eventually become *Greenstone*? That's my hunch. I loved *Greenstone*. So I can't imagine why I would have rejected a book that then became a book I loved.

You just rejected it in its initial form, I suppose.

There's something in my very vague memory that suggests that those two books are linked.

Judith Giblin James suggested that an example of the editor saving the author from herself was your saying a very firm "no" to Sylvia's initial end for Three—**which is the novel about her self-imposed exile, essentially. In the first version of the novel she had**

the son-in-law race on to the tarmac, and tell his mother not to leave, that he wanted her to live with him, that she was the only woman in his life and nothing ... This is clearly fantasy and you said no to this and then she ended it in a way which matched the direction of the novel up to that point. Do you remember that?

Now that you mention it, I do remember it vaguely. I remember thinking it was such a great example of wish-fulfilment but it was clearly not an example of good novel writing and it never would have passed. It wouldn't have passed this way and it wouldn't have passed that way.

I wish my correspondence with her exists. Her letters to me and probably carbons of my letters to her exist, I know ... With all the early letters I was at Simon and Schuster. In early 1968, I went to Knopf, which is the premier literary publishing house in America. When I left I had files as big as this room. I only took two folders of correspondence with me. One was Sylvia's and the other was Joseph Heller's, because it covered *Catch-22* and all sorts of other things. But that correspondence was not as full because Joe lived in New York so we worked together editorially in my office. There would have been memos, there would have been some correspondence, but it wasn't the back and forth I had with Sylvia. I know I have that correspondence. In fact the last few days, knowing I was going to be doing this, I have been looking through my house but it's a four-storey house in New York and I've been in it for 35 years. You can imagine the accumulation of material that both my wife and I have in that house, so I haven't come upon it. If I come upon it, I will alert whoever you want me to alert.

I do want to say something about the strangeness of the relationship we *didn't* have, which was the person-to-person relationship. When she was in New Zealand and I was in Manhattan, there was never even a notion that we would ever meet. When Keith, her husband, died, that was the first time I tried to speak to her. We had never spoken. I'm a telephone guy and I'd be very happy picking up the phone and calling New Zealand even back then when long distance calls were serious. But it never happened. When he died, I called her home to speak to her and she was not able to speak. I don't know whether she was asleep or unable to talk to anyone, but I spoke to one of the boys for five minutes or so and sent my love and attention, etc. That was my first attempt to encounter her directly.

Many years later, as you know, she came to America. I'm not a flyer. I fly a lot more now than I did then. Back when I was flying around the country it somehow never crossed our minds to divert our two itineraries so we could encounter each other. At one stage I was in London and she was in England with Elliot and we realised we were in the same country. And England is not big. It would have been very, very easy to meet and I think I wrote to her and said, "OK here we are. Twenty-five years have gone by and shouldn't we take advantage of this?" She wrote back and said "No I don't think we should. It's been very, very real the way it has been and I don't think I'm prepared at this point to actually meet you." Whether she was nervous that she wouldn't like me or whether she felt it would be too emotional or whether she wasn't happy with the way she looked, I don't know. Since I'm married to an actress wife I can well believe the latter. I don't know why it was, but that was her choice not mine. I guess we came that close and then it didn't happen …

CHAIR: Many thanks, Karl Stead and Robert Gottlieb. Now I understand, Robert, why Sylvia dedicated *Teacher* **to you.**

References

Hood, L. (1988). *Sylvia! The biography of Sylvia Ashton-Warner*. Wellington: Viking.

James, J. G. (2008, August). *"We do things differently behind the Woollen Curtain": Sylvia Ashton-Warner and the education of Robert Gottlieb.* Paper presented at the International Sylvia Ashton-Warner Centennial Conference, The University of Auckland.

Author

Robert Gottlieb has been editor-in-chief of Simon and Schuster, Alfred A. Knopf and *The New Yorker*. He has written extensively for *The New York Review of Books*, *The New Yorker*, *The New York Times Book Review*, and *The New York Observer*. Amongst other well-known publishing achievements, he invented the title *Catch-22*, edited Toni Morrison's work, Chaim Potok's *The Chosen*, John Cheever's posthumous collections, and Bill Clinton's autobiography. He edited eight books by Sylvia Ashton-Warner.

CHAPTER 7

Teaching with Mere: Sylvia Ashton-Warner's 1973 Canadian university class

John Kirkland

Sylvia was invited to take up a teaching position at Simon Fraser University, Vancouver, Canada; she arrived in November 1971 and departed for New Zealand in September 1973. John Kirkland, a New Zealand educationist, recalls the summer he spent in Vancouver assisting Mere (aka Sylvia) as she taught students how to teach using her methods.

In 1973, I was a graduate student from New Zealand studying at University of Missouri's Graduate School. Young, bullet proof and keen to explore North America, I drew up a list of people worth visiting and who might even agree to having my then-wife and me as assistants during a forthcoming summer recess. I had completed course work for a Psychology PhD and my dissertation supervisor was encouraging of my travel plans. This was a once-in-a-lifetime opportunity. Imagine: an entire continent beckoned. Activating this idea was simple: being cheeky enough to send out letters of enquiry.

Spearpoint: 'Teacher' in America (1972) had just been published and its author was a prime candidate, top of the list. I wrote to Sylvia Ashton-Warner care of her New York publishers asking if it might be possible to study "under her" during the summer. This letter was redirected and a fortnight later her reply came from Vancouver: "Your letter came in the morning and the Dean happened to ring me in the evening about the summer workshop and about staff ... I told him I would like you two Kirklands to work with me ..." [1]

Apart from one morning designed to have young children in attendance, this summer school was created for preservice teacher-trainees and included half a dozen Dog Rib students[2] from the Great Slave Lake area, Northwest Territories.

So, along with Cheryl (now Hefford), I worked as a teaching assistant to Sylvia Ashton-Warner for a summer in British Columbia under the banner of Simon Fraser University. The journey to British Columbia turned out to be a much longer drive than expected, literally and figuratively. It was to become a life-changing journey.

---

1 The letter is now archived at the Alexander Turnbull Library, Wellington, New Zealand.
2 A group of First Nations students from the Northwest Territories.

Teaching resources

Sylvia's primary teaching resource was each child's mind. This is neatly expressed by her maxim "Caption the native imagery of our child and use that as working material." But why *native* instead of, say, *personal*, *unique*, *own* or *individual*? I believe *native* brings into focus most directly a cluster of synonyms including *spontaneous, wild, vivid, dynamic, erupting, un-harnessed, uncaptioned, fleeting, savage* and *raw*. This is an artist's reservoir of emotional energy. In direct opposition to *native* there is a suite of words including *crinoline, authority, imposed, power, contained, prescribed* and *tamed*. These are manifestations of Sylvia Ashton-Warner's nemesis: "the establishment". I believe "organic" was introduced into her teaching scheme as part of an overall design with one refrain: "freedom".

Her physical teaching resources included a sand-box and water-box (each measuring about 600 mm x 500 mm x 600 mm, on castors with legs), clean newsprint-paper painting surfaces (on three stand-alone easels) and a clay table. Students also had access to small black-boards. And there was just one low child-sized chair, for her. She'd remark, "We are all at one level in the infant room, on the floor." Apart from a grand piano, all other apartment furniture and furnishings were removed into bedroom storage each workshop day. Unusually, these "Mornings with Young Children" classes were held in her apartment, not at the university. As assistants, our job was to make sure the set-up was completed on time and then after the class tidy up and reposition furniture. It was quite a performance, and exhausting. Even so, I was surprised to find how many extra hours Sylvia put into these classes, especially when preparing illustrated books, drawing on material provided by the Dog Rib students, to whom she took an instant liking.

We called Sylvia "Mere" for a simple reason, namely, "Call me Sylvia if you want the worst of me, Mere if the best." There was no argument. In what follows then, I will refer to Sylvia as Mere, in keeping with her wish.

Guiding Mere's teaching day was a design she had entitled "rhythm of the day". It was depicted as a classic hourglass figure, or a mirrored sine-wave pattern, which she drew on the blackboard[3] (see Figure 1).

Figure 1: Rhythm of the day. (Author's transcription of Sylvia's original.)

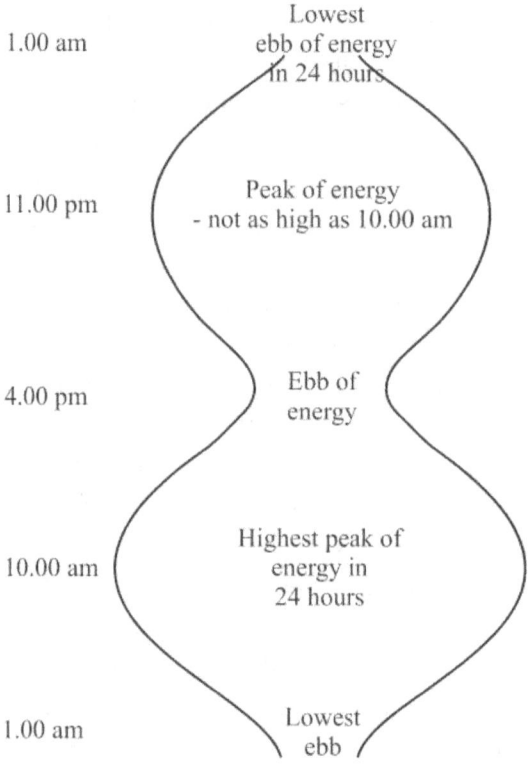

---

3 The original drawing of these figures was given to us on paper by Mere. She drew them on the blackboard, too.

According to Mere, as with diurnal tidal oscillations, a pair of peaks of high nervous energy occurred in the child. Unlike daily tidal time-shifts, these twin peaks were part of what she believed to be fixed circadian patterns, set at 10 am and 11 pm. Superimposed upon this general morning "bulge" was a secondary pattern, pinched into a narrow point at "morning interval" about 10.45 am (see Figure 2).

Figure 2: Shape of the morning. Represented by dashed lines nested within Figure 1.
(Author's transcription of Sylvia's original.)

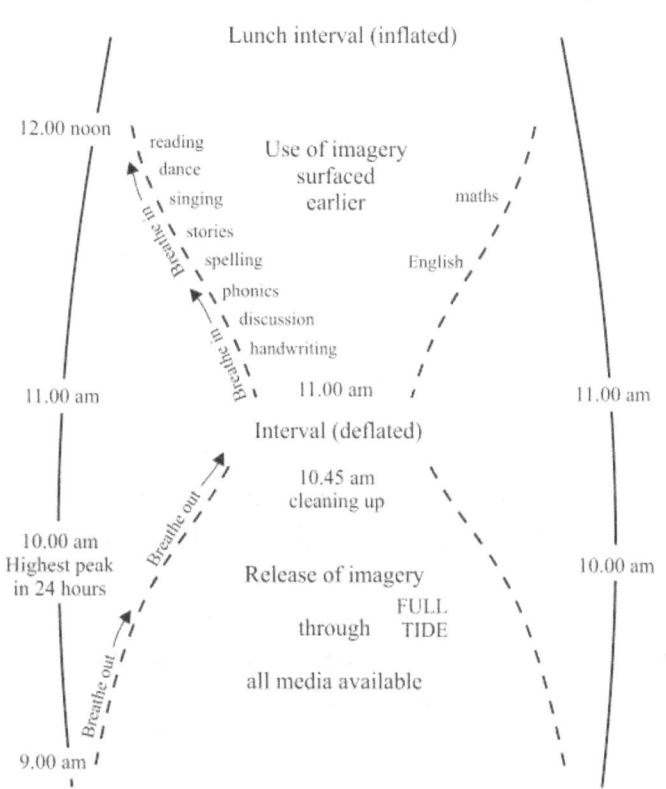

It was Mere's view that "our child" came to school in the morning with energy to spare, at full tide. This is when imagery may be released and all available media are made available for the child's use. It is when Key Vocabulary words bubble to the surface. Any elicited Key Vocabulary words were then "parked" until after morning break. As illustrated in Mere's diagram (Figure 2), it was then that the children's imagery was integrated into other activities like handwriting, discussion, phonics, spelling, reading, playing, singing and dance. Afternoons were reserved for "cultural crafts and skills" including science, nature study and so on. In the classes we never got as far as "afternoons".

Sylvia's teaching methods

It was our habit to kick off our shoes when entering Montecito, which was the name of her apartment. When students arrived on their first day they did likewise. More often than not, when we turned up Mere would be sitting at her grand piano playing softly. We never disturbed this intimate time. We waited unobtrusively until she was ready to welcome us. Each day (Tuesday and Thursday) an action song, such as her creation "Tamariki", would start proceedings. Everybody joined in. Within her rhythm cycle this was part of "breathing out" (Figure 2). It was also a useful period for "settling down" and orienting to what was ahead. Several small cardboard "song-sheets" (about 350 mm x 200 mm) were prepared for guidance, and placed around the floor for easy reading during the group's co-ordinated physical activities, taught by Mere. There was a complete ban on students taking notes during class time, and photography and video recordings were forbidden, too.

Then followed Key Vocabulary work. In these classes, students were encouraged to sit quietly, close their eyes for several minutes and imagine what it was like when they were five-year-olds. Sitting on her little chair Mere would invite a person to come up and sit directly in front, maybe knees-to-knees with her. "Would you like a word? What word would you like?" "Duck" "Would you like me to spell duck for you?"

Holding a piece of unbleached card (about 100 mm x 300 mm), she would spell out slowly, "d-u-c-k", and print these letters very neatly using lower case only. Then she'd take this student's hand and trace over each letter with an index finger, repeating each one simultaneously. "Now, I'm going to ask you if you can see this word. What is this word? Stand to attention, knees together, eyes open, ears open."

The card would be "flashed" twice by flipping it over quickly. When that was done she'd ask what the student would like to do, suggesting playing in sand, painting, water play, clay modelling or blackboard drawing, and off they'd go. This process was repeated for each "child". Few children, she said, would want to do any more writing. To accelerate this process, the students worked in pairs. Just before morning break she'd get everyone into a large circle and allocate clean-up tasks, often seeking out "natural dictators" as temporary leaders to make sure this was done properly.

There was no urgency about this process, no commands, no "must do", no forcing. It was very much like experiencing conditions of relaxed attention which favour development of affection between strangers. As she said, "Provide conditions for life to come in the door, let it." The staging was critical; everything was carefully planned and there was an implicit script to follow, much like an encyclopaedia salesperson's patter. If a person did not have a word to offer when asked there was neither rebuke nor demand. Instead, an invitation was given to go and "play" with available resources. These resources were carefully selected. Conspicuous by their absence were plastic toys and prefabricated materials (like Lego). Sooner or later, as reluctant starters watched their friends participating they'd soon be almost demanding to offer a word too. "A word," she said, "walks hand-in-hand with its image." There was plenty of unhurried time for probing gently to release this "native imagery". Those familiar with de Saint Exupéry's (1967) delightful tale of the fox will recognise the essential and parallel characteristics of "taming".

After morning-break time, there would be "input", breathing in. During this phase, previously "parked" drawn-out imagery was revisited in a structured way. Mere would take that pile of Key Vocabulary words and scatter them around, inviting people to "Now, find your own word."

Once they had found their words, the students (children) each took a small blackboard and piece of chalk. They would sit on their boards, arranged into a semicircle around Mere's little chair while she spoke about the Key Vocabulary words. She'd choose one word. "Now, here's *duck*. Ask your neighbour questions about this duck. What colour is it? Was it flying? Was it dead?" The students talked about *duck*, using spoken words to generate many images. After a series of questions, the students wrote words onto their own small boards using a nondominant hand to get a feel of what a 5-year-old's fine-motor co-ordination might be like. This writing led naturally enough on to organic vocabulary, organic reading, organic discussion and stories. All of this started from within.

Some people should not try

In my view some people should not even try to apply the Key Vocabulary. In Sylvia Ashton-Warner's terms, teaching is a dangerous activity and children need protection from certain people. I would include here most scholarly academics, as they often lack what I believe is an essential balance of capability, temperament and knowledge in this intimate context. To do this job well requires meeting at least four basic criteria.

First, a person would need to have already experienced a wide spectrum of both dark and light emotions deeply and have a capacity to explore and report about these experiences coherently. That is, being able to give feelings words. This is a worldly knowledge seasoned by experience and generally unfamiliar to those under age 25. It links directly into an appreciation of how "art", interpreted broadly and including music, is generated from feelings and can be communicated to resonate in others.

Second, a Key Vocabulary teacher would need natural warmth of personality. This would radiate as unthreatening care along with unending patience to foster personal, social and community development.

Third, as this is a complex scheme, its understanding and application demands relatively high intelligence. "Thinking intelligence" is needed, and practitioners may glean and interpret what is relevant in this regard from *Teacher* (1966) and *Spinster* (1958). "Practical intelligence" is required too. The practice of the Key Vocabulary involves high-performance multitasking, including setting out equipment, managing a special learning environment, reviewing reflectively each child's "progress" and recording this evolution according to a basic and evolving plan.

Finally, it is necessary to have a sense of adventure and humour coupled with resilience and continuing professional self-development. These four characteristics all need to be embedded in a thorough familiarity with Sylvia Ashton-Warner's "four-movement" reading-scheme (see below) and its fundamental relationship to music, rhythm and physical contact. Whether or not a person is a trained teacher is irrelevant.

The "four-movement" reading scheme

Applying a musical analogy, Mere's teaching scheme was arranged into four separate "movements". Everything in her pedagogical engagement was connected; that is to say everything was a working-out of an implicit musical grammar. One time she confided how her little stories were designed and crafted. She said she would unpack a little-known sonata (from, say, Beethoven) to identify how emotional nuances could be conveyed through cadences, rhythms and general overall structure. Then she would use that "form" as a frame for organising her own content. "Why," she asked rhetorically, "should I try to create a pattern when the Masters have done this already?" It was her understanding of musical grammar that allowed her to undertake these creative transformations. They were translations; intermodal variations on particular themes, and undoubtedly a sign of her genius. Many of her delightful stories and accompanying musical scores are available in *O Children of the World* (Ashton-Warner, 1974).

Here is a brief summary of Mere's "four-movement" scheme. Further details are available in *Teacher* (1966) and *Spinster* (1958), as well as various published articles. Knowing how the movements flow into one another to move a child along in a timely manner across various transitions is "curriculum knowledge". To be able successfully to follow Mere's scheme means having familiarity with principles of design and style, a working knowledge of dynamic psychology and a sense of rhythm. An abiding sense of rhythm (be this seasonal, monthly, weekly, daily or immediate as in music) is critical for understanding "flow".

> *Movement one:* Key Vocabulary. The child's selected words were printed onto white strip-cards, with the child's name on the reverse. No illustrations and no drawings were added because word images (that is, the word accompanied by its intimate and bound imagined referent) are vivid; they exist in the child's mind's eye and are drawn from intense feelings such as fears and loves.
>
> *Movement two:* More words. Again, printed neatly by a teacher in lower case, onto hole-punched coloured strip-cards. These words start to emerge when the Key Vocabulary has been exhausted; they are also spontaneous.

Movement three: Recontextualising words. There are three distinct sequential subphases (first-, second-, third-movement books have covers in different shades of blue, each mapping on to a child's developing writing competencies): A teacher writes words onto a blue card and child copies these into the relevant book that is line ruled to accommodate each child's ability to print neatly. Book one (light blue, measuring about 220 mm x 100 mm) has five stapled pages of unlined newsprint paper (see free-books, below). Book two (mid-blue, also about 220 mm x 100 mm) has five pages, each with three equally spaced lines. Words are printed onto the middle line. Book three (deeper blue colour, about 220 mm x 120 mm) has eight pages of regularly lined paper. Each entry has two lines for each, letters occupying the full line width and extending to upper and lower lines as necessary (with *b* or *j*, for instance).

Movement four: Children's writing. Here each child works alone with a green-covered booklet (about 220 mm x 140 mm) that has around eight lined pages, spine stapled. Again, as with the blue book, movement three, only alternative lines are used so that printing occupies full interline spaces.

Other handmade books

Three further sorts of handmade booklets were developed from the four-movement process outlined above. I suspect these were added to fill in gaps and expand on this four-step "natural" process.

- *Free-books:* These were stapled booklets whose content was "free" from constraint and expressed the spontaneous imagination of the child. These booklets illustrated the mind's images, and drew out feelings. To make the books, at movement three (book one) the teacher selected key sentences with the child's new words. The words were copied, and illustrated by the teacher. Illustrations were photocopied and the child coloured these.

- *Key Vocabulary books:* These were booklets made of teacher-copied words, copied from Key Vocabulary slips and printed at odd angles, one per page, onto blank pages, coloured-card covered and spine stapled.
- *Trans-cultural books:* These books are parallel to the above but have two languages displayed, in this instance English and an Athapaskan language of the Dog Rib people. The idea of "trans-cultural" reading was important to Mere, and she'd written memos and other documents to advance it. I believe this encounter with Dog Rib students was her first outside New Zealand with non-English speakers. On several occasions she took the Dog Rib students aside and they worked hard outside of scheduled class time to make the "trans-cultural" books. In this particular "class", five "Key Vocabulary" booklets were produced; each showed both languages for single words expressing "loves" and "fears". In addition, there were two sets of English-only "free-books"; eight called *Bay sa Kwo*, and three named *Sia-Kon*. Figure 3 shows a free-book page with a line-drawing illustration by Sylvia Ashton-Warner's own hand.

Assessment

Mere had disdain for grading people. As a consequence, in her classes course grading was by self-assessment. She wrote out a set of questions: Who is the musician who composes for you? Who is the best poet you like? Quote 20 lines from any poem. Which artist has had the greatest influence on you? How many artists do you know? Name both thought and feeling currents of last two centuries. When was Buddha born? Do you giggle when people are being serious? Do you have dreams that lure you on? Name one person who has had the greatest impact on your life.

There are certain parallels here with Frank McCourt's unusual grading approach when he asks, "First, how was your attendance?

Figure 3: Sylvia Ashton-Warner's hand-drawn illustration for a Bay sa Kwo booklet.
(From author's copy of Sylvia's course-related work produced at Simon Fraser University summer school, 1973.)

Even if you sat quietly in the back and thought about the discussions and readings, you surely learned something. Second, did you participate? Did you get up there and read on Fridays? Anything. Stories, essays, poetry, plays. Third, did you comment on the work of your classmates? Fourth, and this is up to you, can you reflect on this experience and ask yourself what you learned? Fifth, did you just sit there and dream? If you did, give yourself credit" (2005, p. 253). McCourt's style is reminiscent of *Teacher*. Both teacher–authors display an astute ear for dialogue, provide extremely personalised accounts, write with spontaneity and pepper their text with aphorisms.

Finally ...

To create a summary of my observations of Mere's "teacher training" that summer at her apartment in Vancouver, I offer some remarks about the idea of *drawing*. Mere often commented that everything started by "dipping into a child's mind" to seek and find "raw material". This reaching in was designed to release native imagery, that is, to *draw from* what is within while retaining the child's organic spirit.

Through applying Mere's carefully orchestrated "teaching methods" (she did not believe she *taught*, which was a much too formal word for her own practices), this raw material becomes transformed into communicable patterns (words), achieved by *drawing* feelings *alongside* and *into* a particular culture's wordless forms. In short, this is a matter of nurturing nature so as to reorganise each child's imaginative source material into recognisable, communicable patterns, all the while retaining the child's spontaneous, vivid imagery. Activities such as hand drawing, dance and music become important because they occupy the indeterminate time zone between native imagery and its possible representations. Captioned imagery may eventually be *drawn down* and *drawn into* more fixed representations such as writing and speech. It is all that straightforward.

For Mere, numeracy and literacy are end points of a long "drawn-out process", and she showed us the place to start from—but her educational approach probably requires the wisdom of Solomon, the patience of Job, the understanding of Freud, and the flair of an artist. That summer in Vancouver I came to believe that Mere had this rare combination of qualities—and that maybe these qualities are not easily drawn out of us as teachers.

References

Ashton-Warner, S. (1958). *Spinster*. London: Secker & Warburg.

Ashton-Warner, S. (1963). *Teacher*. New York: Simon & Schuster.

Ashton-Warner, S. (1972). *Spearpoint: 'Teacher' in America*. New York: Knopf.

Ashton-Warner, S. (1974). *O children of the world: Songs and stories*. Vancouver: First Person Press.

de Saint Exupéry, A. (1967). *The little prince*. Harmondsworth, England: Penguin.

McCourt, F. (2005). *Teacher man*. London: Fourth Estate.

Author

John Kirkland was born in Temuka, New Zealand, and stepped from small-farm life into academia. He gained a PhD in Psychology from the University of Missouri, 1976. John taught at Simon Fraser University with Sylvia Ashton-Warner (summer of 1973); was a lecturer at University of London (1974–6), and has been at Massey University in New Zealand since 1976. His current academic interests are learning recovery, developmental theory (particularly attachment), and designing interesting courses.
Email: J.Kirkland@massey.ac.nz

CHAPTER 8

Sylvia Ashton-Warner and Māori children: "I do not think Sylvia learned much from the kids"

Merimeri Penfold

As a new young Māori teacher, Merimeri Penfold (Ngāti Kurī) taught at Waiomatatini for one year in 1945, while Sylvia was there. In this edited transcript of an interview with Alison Jones,[1] Merimeri tells a story of her own radical teaching, describes the context within which Sylvia taught, and gives a sense of how some Māori saw Sylvia. Merimeri was raised speaking her own language in the rural Māori community of Te Hapua in the far north of New Zealand.

---

1 Merimeri Penfold talked to Alison Jones on 6 November 2008.

For me, language is everything. As a kid, I was fascinated by the English language as delivered by my Pākehā teachers. They spoke so precisely! We used to copy them; we were like magpies. We would go around and pretend to be the teacher. And we were very laboured in our use of the English language. We could not be as precise using English sounds as the Pākehā teachers could be in their language. We would cope with this dual linguistic exercise, and we became pretty good at it. We used to go home, and practise and use the phrases used by Pākehā teachers, like "excuse me" and "pardon me" and "What on earth are you doing?" We would be clipped around the ears because our parents banned us from speaking English at home: "Don't use that language in this house!" At school it was: "Do not speak Māori in this place!" The parents were on the outside of the school, they were not participants. They suspected the Pākehā tika [way]; they would not come to school—but we kids were free agents. We could go between both worlds.

Linguistically, we kids grew to be smart. We played around with the languages when we were away from home and from school, and we developed a facility with both. We enjoyed it. It was a challenge, and we would have a go and be prepared to be punished for it. But we were not bitter about this, not like students today, they become very bitter about it. It is true that some kids were not stimulated by having the two languages in the home and the school. English hurt their ears. They would block their ears. The high pitch of the Pākehā teacher's voice was a physically painful thing—it was so different from the easier, lower Māori sound.

Sylvia at Waiomatatini

I went to Waiomatatini in 1945. It was a very isolated place. Keith Henderson was the headmaster there, and Sylvia was Infant Mistress. Bob Kerr (a Pākehā) and his wife Bea (who was Tainui) were there, and a local girl whose name was Pare Maurirere. When I arrived I looked around and I thought Pare was the Infant Mistress because she was always there. But as the weeks went by it turned out that the Infant Mistress did not come to school until about 10.30 for morning tea! She would come and sit down and ask Bea for a cup of tea. Bea would say "Well, help yourself." I would not have been able to say what she said.

Sylvia was not at the school a lot. I did not view her as a serious teacher, and she was not a role model for me because she came and went as she pleased. We had staff meetings with Keith, all about running the school—for instance, kids were playing marbles (Bob Kerr was a crack shot at marbles and he used to play with the kids and win all the marbles, and the kids would come the next day to get them back) and the kids started to gang up against each other … Those were the sorts of issues for the staff meetings. But Sylvia was never at any meeting that I remember. She arrived as a sort of fashion model in our midst for us to gaze on.

The art work that Sylvia developed when I was at Waiomatatini was clay modelling. The kids would scrape the mud on the window panes and wipe the clay off their hands on the desks. There was clay everywhere! In those days, the policy in the rural schools was that the Department of Education would supply all the teaching materials, and in return the senior kids would clean the school—they emptied the toilets, they polished the school, and tidied the playground. Every afternoon, there were regular jobs. It was a healthy process, they learnt how to handle things. So after Sylvia's clay-modelling period the senior kids had to slosh and sweep the whole classroom out. The classrooms were opened out to the air. Poor Pare had to keep the kids outside so the classroom could dry out! Pare was the one who told us all about the clay.

When Sylvia finally arrived at school in the morning she addressed the children using certain chords on the piano. No words! A chord for "Stand up, children", another for "You may go outside now" …

hardly any spoken word. Everyone recognised the chord for "Good morning". She would sometimes also say "Good morning" but she was dependent on the piano rather than her voice in that situation. She was a terrific pianist. She made wonderful paintings on the classroom wall. She was an artist more than she was a teacher. Every time she played the piano, they loved it, they all listened—even in my classroom. They would say "whakarongo, whakarongo! [listen!]". It was beautiful, but it was erratic.

I did not speak to Sylvia much at all because she did not speak to people. She did not engage with the local Māori community when I was there. I think her idea about teaching that became famous was just a germ of an idea at that time in Waiomatatini; it had not yet developed. When I heard later that she had a theory about teaching Māori children to read I thought it must be about Māori language teaching, but that was not so. I am not sure whether she knew how to speak Māori; it was not apparent to me then, anyway. If she had these ideas about teaching Māori children I would have thought she would have asked us, talked to us, but she did not. Was she really so concerned about Māori children?

She was elusive; you couldn't get near her. I found myself calling her a tūrehu, a fairy, because she was silent most of the time, and she looked very fair, with a pointed nose, lovely eyes … very self-contained. She did not talk to the locals. They were mataku of her; afraid of her. She was a free spirit, floating around. That was the way she was.

Pākehā and Māori

Sylvia reminded me of my first Pākehā, the first Pākehā I ever saw, as a kid. I was delivering the milk to the headmaster. I went with my blue can after we had milked the cows. I walked to the school house. It was a huge house, a magnificent place. There was a knob on the door, a brass knob, a beautiful knob. I stood and admired it; I was all eyes! I knocked at the door, the door opened and there was this kuia [old woman]—with gray hair, pointy nose, blue eyes, she was tiny. I stood and looked at her. She had small feet. My one ambition was to have small feet; I did not have small feet because I had never worn shoes. This is how I regarded her, this first Pākehā I had seen: as an old kuia. She was distant, a fairy, a tūrehu. When I look back on it, it was a strange sort of experience.

I do not think Sylvia learned much from the kids because she was rarely among the kids. Apirana Ngata's marae [community meeting place] was not far from the school. That was where the kids were being influenced, but she did not work with the people from there. She could say the different Māori names of the kids like Hiria and Wharepapa. When she said those words they did not jar for me, so she could pronounce Māori okay. She was relaxed about it and was good at it, and accepted the children's names. She did not change the names into Pākehā words, which was a tradition amongst the Pākehā teachers. I am Merimeri but when I went to school I become Mary; my father Rapata became Robert, and so on. She did not do that.

Keith did not speak Māori. It was unusual for Pākehā headmasters at that time to speak Māori, even in Māori areas. We Māori teachers were able to meet with the parents, talk to them in Māori. We would speak to people like Hiria's grandmother; she was very quiet, an old woman. She liked to know her moko [grandchild] was doing well.

Māori teachers

I was in the first wave of Māori teachers to be trained and to go into the schools, in the early 1940s. Because we were native speakers we could hold our own in a way that the next generation, who could not speak Māori, could not. They did not have the confidence we had. Language was something that was not a problem for us. The next generation came from households where the parents spoke Māori to each other, but spoke English to the kids. The lack of confidence went on through their teaching lives, but as they developed their language they became more mature, and they could use the language to challenge the system, and to campaign to have Māori taught in the school system.

When I was a teacher, the children spoke Māori at home. But in the classroom I spoke only English to the children. That is the way it was; it was something the system threw us into. Māori-speaking teachers came out of Teachers' Training College believing that we were to do that. When I went to Te Whāiti, the country area, there was Maurice Bird up in Ruatāhuna, Sid Mead was in the same area—these teachers were Māori-speaking and all the kids were Māori speaking. We were all under the same ruling: no Māori to be spoken. There we were—the *fools* that we were! Had to abide by the ruling! I resented it. I was a native speaker, the kids were native speakers and here we were communicating in another language. We had to get somewhere, and we realised that these kids had to learn to speak English. But it involved denying them their language in the classroom. When the children went outside the classroom, when they were playing games, they were speaking Māori all the time.

So I rebelled. It was humiliating to be under that system. The school inspector was due in six weeks. I thought, okay, I will now play a different language game. I decided that during the development period first thing in the morning, when the children spoke about things that interested them, we would speak in Māori. From my experience, when we spoke in English as usual, I noticed it was the Pākehā kids that dominated every morning. They were usually always the first up, and the Māori kids would immediately go to sleep, couldn't be bothered listening. The Māori kids were in agony; it was registered in their faces; they were miserable. When you looked at them you could see their eyes were heavy, and they lacked any light in their eyes. So, I said: "Me kōrero Māori tātou;

kōrero mai. [Speak Māori everyone; speak up]". When the Māori kids were asked to speak in English, the things they said were simple and repetitive: "Last night when I went home I got in my working clothes, and I played". That's all they would say! But when it came to "kōrero mai" you couldn't get them to shut up. They touched on all sorts of topics: going with their father to split posts for fences; going with their father to tickle trout; catching eels …

I was cutting across the unwritten ruling that Māori was not to be spoken in the classroom. But the kids' eyes would become bright! After a child spoke to the class I would say "He pātai? [any questions?]" and the questions would come, in Māori: "Who went pig-hunting with you?" "My dog". Then some of the kids would say "E hoa, don't lie!" The child was only small; he must have had a father or brother with him. Sure enough: "Tāku Pāpā [my father]". Then: "What is the name of your dog?" They all knew the answer, but they liked the game of asking questions. When they used the language they played with it, they grew and they looked healthy. They were brilliant to watch. But of course, the eyes of the Pākehā kids who did not know the language were now dull. They were not with it. The talking development period from then on was a fantastic experience—the Māori children would participate. They enjoyed it like when they were playing rugby.

We used to have interschool sports. The children from Ruatāhuna would come down and the children and parents would mihi [greet] each other; we were the tangata whenua [host people] so we would mihi and karanga [welcome] them. The school kids were doing the tikanga Māori [Māori custom], and the manuhiri [visitors] would respond back in Māori, all done beautifully, and they would tease each other, saying: "We will feed you up so you will not be able to run fast"—it was a wonderful and spirited exchange.

Struggle

When the school inspector came I said to him, "Look, I have prepared a programme. I would like you to sit and observe how the children behave and react." He was coming to observe me; I wanted him to look at the children as well. Anyway, we started in English as was expected, and the Pākehā kids took over, and asked all the questions too. Then, "Kei a koutou, kōrero mai, kōrero mai", I said, it is your time now. There were three kids crowding up to speak, and the rest were leaning forward. They were all ready to show off. Māori kids love to show off in an element they can handle. The inspector must have been able to see the enthusiasm of these kids who had been sitting there like doormats or doornails. They went on and on, and I had to ask them to sit down to let others have a chance or some would talk all the time. The children were challenging the speaker, asking questions. Sometimes the kids showed how they used Māori and English languages together. One boy said "Ka haere mai tāku Pāpā ka kikia up the backside [My father came to kick me up the backside]." I said in Māori, "Pahiri, use the right words." So he said it properly in Māori. Then another boy was talking about chasing a pig and how it was killed, and how they singed it. All the other kids were excited and trying to ask questions because they were interested in the drama of the pig being killed, and being singed, and the dog getting lost ...

It was exhausting, trying to control them! I had never before experienced that sort of struggle with young kids, when I was a teacher using English language. When the children were passionate about their topic and were allowed to speak in their own language, they revelled in it. They spoke with confidence, and felt *so* confident—*the world was theirs.*

And that showed me that colonialism knocked the confidence out of the tangata whenua [the indigenous people] by hitting the language. Saying to the people over generations: learn this other language, leave your own language. My own people at Te Hapua became a lost group of people. As a result of this loss of confidence and their own language not being used, they suspected the system, they suspected the schools, they suspected the health system, they did not want to have their babies at the hospital because they did not know how that system would behave with them. The rot in the system came in when it was declared "forget about your past. Elements of your past, they are taonga [valuable], but give them away…" That left my people in a cultural desert. I can see this now, looking back, so clearly in my classroom.

After he had watched my class, the inspector and I had a long talk. He said "Yes, I noticed the young kids came to life, they looked healthy, their skins shone, they were bright-eyed, eager"… eagerness he did not see at all before in the eyes of these kids. The contrast was such that he could not help notice. But he said, "Mrs Penfold, you are aware that it is not the written policy of the department that Māori be spoken in school".[2]

For me, the ultimate is the language, te reo Māori. Sylvia did not do that work.

References

Barrington, J. (2008). *Separate but equal? Māori schools and the Crown, 1867–1969.* Wellington: Victoria University Press.

Simon, J. (Ed.). (1998). *Ngā kura Māori: The native schools system 1867–1969.* Auckland: Auckland University Press.

Simon, J., & Tuhiwai Smith, L. (Eds.). (2001) *A civilising mission? Perceptions and representations of the Native Schools system.* Auckland: Auckland University Press.

---

2   The Native Schools Act 1867 that established schools for Māori in rural areas stated that instruction was to be in English "as far as practicable". This policy was followed (or not) in various ways until the disestablishment of Native Schools in the 1960s. For discussion of the policy, practices and the experiences of Māori language in Native Schools, see Simon (1998), Simon & Tuhiwai Smith (2001, pp. 141ff) and John Barrington (2008).

Author

Merimeri (Meremere) Penfold (Ngāti Kurī) taught Māori language at The University of Auckland for more than 30 years. She has been a member of the Māori Education Foundation, a Human Rights Commissioner, and an executive member of the New Zealand Broadcasting Commission—amongst many other things. Dr Penfold also worked on the seventh edition of H. W. Williams' *Dictionary of Maori Language*. She undertook the first translation of Shakespeare's love sonnets into Māori *(Ngā waiata aroha a Hekepia,* published by Holloway Press, The University of Auckland in 2000). Merimeri was made a Companion of the New Zealand Order of Merit for services to Māori in 2001, and has been for many years kaumatua (elder) of The University of Auckland.

CHAPTER 9

Learning without teaching: Sylvia Ashton-Warner's classroom as a seed for kōhanga reo

Iritana Tawhiwhirangi

Iritana Tawhiwhirangi (Ngāti Porou[1]) was one of the founders of the kōhanga reo movement in New Zealand. The kōhanga reo—"language nest"—is a total-immersion Māori-language family programme for young children from birth to six years. First established in 1982, kōhanga reo now form a significant sector of the early childhood education system in New Zealand. Iritana taught in Sylvia's classroom at Waiomatatini in 1948. In this edited transcript of an interview with Alison Jones,[2] Iritana talks about how Sylvia became an inspiration for some key elements of the kōhanga reo.

---

1 Iritana Tawhiwhirangi's tribal affiliations and ancestry are Ngāti Porou as well as Ngā Puhi and Ngāti Kahungunu, English and Canadian. She was brought up on the East Coast speaking both Māori and English.
2 Iritana Tawhiwhirangi talked to Alison Jones on 9 December 2008.

In 1948 I went to Waiomatatini as a relieving teacher for Sylvia Ashton-Warner. At the school, they were having trouble with her because she was spending less time at school than she ought to. So they brought me in to relieve in the Infant Mistress position for three months. Sylvia was with me in her classroom for brief periods, depending on whether she was in the mood to come over to the school. At the beginning she came quite a bit, but as she thought I had a handle on her style of operating she came less frequently, and left me on my own. I was only 19 years old, and fresh out of teachers' college.

Originally, I had no intention of being a teacher; I just wanted to avoid being a nurse! The Wellington Teachers' College was so sterile and restricted,[3] with its obsession with order and rules, and bells ringing. I came from a childhood environment that was free and open and alive, and here was an institution closed down, narrowed down, regimented; I hated it.

I came straight out of that rigid environment into Sylvia's classroom. It was so different from what I had been trained to do, I was shell-shocked at first. It was confusing for me. But I noticed how the kids responded; they loved it. And it was more like what I was used to, growing up. There was chaos and, you might say, not a lot of teaching; but at the same time, intensive learning was going on.

Learning without teaching

Sylvia did not talk much, not even in the classroom. She did not teach. That is, she did not *instruct*. She had the children talking to each other, and asking her questions, or she would ask them questions. Her classroom was like a home, or a marae [community meeting place]. It was not rigid or overly formal; everyone just got on with it and interacted with each other naturally. She did not issue instructions

---

3   Interestingly, although it may not have been evident to many of the students, Wellington Teachers' College was a centre of Progressive Education during the 1930s to 1950s. See Middleton & May (1997).

all the time. The kids knew what to do. I remember this boy coming in with muddy gumboots and she went to the piano and played a few chords, and he said "Oh, yes" and went outside and took off his boots! There was a piano connection to what she was saying and the children understood it.

The riverbed was just down from the school, so she had the children building tunnels and building things with sticks. Most of the kids would never have been to a town and would not have seen a tunnel. But she got them to build one so they could talk about tunnels. They would make aeroplanes with sticks, and fly them down to the imaginary airport. The sheep would be having lambs, and she would take them across to see the sheep and lambs, and get the kids all excited. She would then bring them back to the classroom and sit them on the floor and say "Now, who is going to tell me a story about what they saw today?" The thing that struck me was that she could teach all age groups at once. There were new entrants (aged 5) up to Standard 2 (aged 8) in the classroom. She would say "How do we start a story?" They would call out "A capital letter!" (She never had "big letters, small letters". It was all the proper language; she never used baby talk.) She wrote the stories up as the children were saying them. The littlies who could not write yet would draw pictures. She was able to tailor what was happening to the learning level of the children, the point they were at. The little ones learned as they went, watching and following the older ones, just like at the marae.

The kids would use good language. They would say, for example, "Miss Henderson, she was flying across the paddock." They were observant; they took in everything, and rich language came out of that.

Parents at school

Many of the parents and nannies were there at the school all day. I am not sure whether it was because they were worried about their children with this odd teacher, or whether Keith Henderson, the headmaster, had asked them to come, or whether Sylvia encouraged them herself, but when I was at the school it was normal for the parents and old people to come to school with their children. It was an open classroom, and they sat outside and watched what was going on. The children would run out to their nanny with their work to show them the work they had done.

The parents thought she was odd, but they were impressed with what she managed to do with the children. They would take books and teaching materials home. She had cards with the number combinations and concepts on them; she had all this equipment. She had made them up herself; there were no shops for buying things to teach with. The parents would see the children working with the cards and take the cards home, like homework. Because the parents were there watching how the cards worked, they could help their kids at home.

The parents were in and out of the classroom, they would walk through or sit and watch but they never got in the way. They would sit by the door, sit with the kids. It was open. There was no thought that they should not be there; and there was no thought that they would take over the classroom—which is what some teachers are worried about. Sylvia did not go to any trouble over the parents. They felt comfortable and welcome in the classroom, and they were learning alongside their children. They found it interesting, what was going on. It was a social get-together for them as well. It was like a marae; people were learning. They could get involved if they wanted to or not, but they understood what is going on.

Really, this was the seed for the kōhanga reo movement. For me, the most important thing was involving the whānau [extended family]. There was no parent engagement in the schools at the time. As I saw it, parents were locked out of the classroom and out of their children's education. I saw children being left behind and not catching up because they did not stay up with the class, and yet they could not get the help from home because their home was shut out. That was the seed: when I saw Sylvia's school I saw parents wanting to take material home from the school to help their children, because the parents were there and could see when their children were struggling, and they wanted to help. The parents could understand what their children were having to do. This was my model for the kōhanga reo; classrooms should open their doors to parents.

The other thing that inspired me in my work getting the kōhanga movement going was the way that Sylvia made learning joyful. Make learning a joyful experience, that's my greatest message for the kōhanga. Sylvia's classroom, the kids loved it; they would come running in the morning.

Māori language

People have pointed out that Sylvia did not teach the children in Māori. The fact is, at that time in the 1940s, the language was not an issue. The children were getting good Māori language at home, and good English from school, so language was not a problem. Māori language was very strong in the home, and the parents could also speak English.

The story of discouraging children for speaking their language in schools is an interesting one. In 1939, when I was about 10 years old, I heard Apirana Ngata speak at our marae in Hicks Bay [on the East Coast]. Apirana Ngata was the guru of Māoridom; he was from the East Coast, and he had Department of Education officials with him, travelling up the coast talking about schooling. To this day I remember very clearly what he said. It stuck in my head. He said: "I want you to teach my people English, English, and more English."

Our old people were sitting there listening to this—and they *listened* to him, they listened to anything and everything he said—and they began to speak a pidgin form of English. They started saying things like "key the door", "broom the floor". Here was this precious new thing that Apirana had put such importance on: English. So they all tried to speak it. I was amused when my nannies used to switch into this funny language.

So the reason why kids were being discouraged by the Department of Education from speaking English at school was because here was this demigod from Māoridom telling them to teach English—so they would teach it come what may, so they did not get into trouble with the Māori leader.

The problem was that the people thought that in order to teach English you had to stop teaching or speaking Māori. That was an error. The spinoff was disastrous, and the effects continue to this day.

So I do not blame the teachers in Sylvia's time for not encouraging Māori language in school. That is what the community wanted.

Sylvia flashed through my life like a sort of shooting star. But in the brief period I was with her, she left an impact on me that has stayed with me throughout my life.

Reference

Middleton, S., & May, H. (1997). *Teachers talk teaching 1915–1995: Early childhood, schools and teachers' colleges.* Palmerston North: Dunmore Press.

Author

Iritana Tawhiwhirangi (née Thatcher) MBE CNZM, Ngāti Porou/ Kahungunu/Ngā Puhi/Canadian/English affiliations. Iritana Tawhiwhirangi is seen as a "cornerstone" of the kōhanga reo (Māori language programme for infants) movement. She taught with Sylvia Ashton-Warner at Waiomatatini in 1948 where, she says, she developed some principles for the kōhanga reo. She has served

on a host of government committees involved in the development of education policy. She is currently a member of Te Kōhanga Reo National Trust Board, as well as active in many other organisations. Iritana was granted an honorary Doctorate of Literature from Victoria University of Wellington in 2007.
Email: iritana@kohanga.ac.nz

CHAPTER 10

Memories of my mother

Elliot Henderson

Sylvia and Keith Henderson had three children: Jasmine, Elliot and Ashton. These memories, written by Elliot Henderson, are excerpted from a longer account called "Memoirs of Sylvia Ashton-Warner", an unpublished manuscript circulated to the International Sylvia Ashton-Warner Centennial Conference at The University of Auckland, New Zealand, 9–10 August 2008.

Sylvia 1

I recall one of my first conversations with Sylvia. I was 3 years old. Between the school house at Pipiriki and the school was a disused tennis court, at the end of which was a clay bank. On this bank Sylvia was sculpting a full-sized horse. I gazed at the finished work in wonderment. It seemed quite amazing and perfect—the muscles in the neck, the mane, the sinewy legs. Out of my awe at this creation came a troubled question: "But what happens when the rains come?" "Well—it will be washed away, dear."

As I pondered her reply, I came to the conclusion that I was in the presence of a very strange person. Why, I thought, would she go to so much trouble to create this beautiful creature only to have it disappear in the first rainstorm. I decided that either she must be mad, or she had a way of seeing creation which I could not understand. I wondered if other mothers were like this. But there weren't any other mothers to compare her with.

Sylvia 2

Pipiriki had several aspects to it. There was work to begin with. For Sylvia, work meant her own writing. For Keith, work meant his professional career as a teacher and headmaster.

Sylvia found that, given the exigencies of her work as a teacher and the requirements of her family, particularly the children, the only time to write would be before school. So she would get up early in the morning to do this. This pattern remained with her all her life.

Then there was the family. Again, Sylvia would set aside a time in the morning before school to spend time with the children. Then, too, there was her music. She played a lot of Beethoven and Schubert and Chopin—particularly Schubert, who was, probably, the great love of her life. I don't remember much Mozart. She would practise these in the morning, along with her writing and her time with the children.

In Pipiriki, Sylvia met Joy Alley, the district nurse, who lived down the road. Sylvia was a person of very strong feeling. From time to time, there was someone like Joy who became the recipient of Sylvia's natural instinct to form a passionate friendship. Presumably, she could discuss with Joy those longings of the heart which she was not able to with anyone else. Again, such a relationship became a pattern in her life. There were many variations of it. And it was not necessarily a woman. Men, too, were often the recipients of her passionate friendship.

Which brings us to the other important strand—Selah. Her Selah was a place, outside the house, but not too far from it, where she could go, to be alone, and to do her work. The children became quite accustomed to this. Often, when we went to a new school, and a new school house, the three children would rush around to choose the most suitable room. And then, there would be the question: "Where will Selah be?"

Sylvia 3

We must have gone to Pipiriki about the beginning of 1942. I would have been about 5 then, so I began my schooling in my mother's classroom. Ashton was still a toddler, but he was brought along too. Some of the bigger girls would look after him. I learned my numbers. Sylvia had a pattern of numbers drawn in colours—two lots of five stacked on top of each other with the three and the eight in the middle of each five. The three was blue the four was yellow and the five probably red. The seven may well have been orange, but whenever I think of numbers now I always bring this image to mind.

They were the years of war, of course. There was a general sense of menace about what was happening overseas. Every evening we would listen to the news on the radio followed by the BBC Radio newsreel with its familiar introductory music—some stirring and attractive band music. I was still listening to that at university. As Keith sat listening to the radio with cigarette smoke curling above his head we were told that the mosquitoes had attacked some targets. I couldn't understand why the world should care about being attacked by mosquitoes. It all seemed quite odd—particularly as Keith looked rather grave. Mosquitoes did not seem very threatening to me.

There were visitors from Wellington, mainly relatives. Ostensibly they were escaping the threat of a Japanese invasion. But the simple rural charms of Pipiriki were not enough to keep them long, and most went back to their cities, preferring, I imagine, to face the Japanese. Around the school, deep trenches had been dug. Exactly what they were for escapes me still. If we were going to hide from the Japanese we could easily go into the forest. But there were schemes to chop down trees to stop any invading traffic on the roads. I thought it unlikely that Pipiriki would figure very large in the strategic Japanese plan.

Sylvia would regularly disappear, either to go to Selah, or to go to see Joy. We were forbidden to go to Joy's house. I do not recall much warmth from her towards the children. She was somewhat remote. Her face was finely sculptured and handsome in an aristocratic way. But there was a distance, a kind of *hauteur*—at least towards the children. When Sylvia died, she sent us a simple flower tribute with genuine words of warmth.

Sylvia 4

During her first year in Pipiriki, from February 1941, Sylvia wrote a diary. The entries appeared haphazardly at different intervals. There are some scenes of family life, but a lot of the diary was given over to the development of her relationship with Joy Alley. She published the diary under the title *Myself*, in 1966, 25 years later. At the end of her introduction (i.e., her address to her readers) she explains why she has left in the friendship with Joy. Since it is supposed to be a book about her early experiences as a teacher she has to give a reason for this friendship's occupying such a large portion of the book: "As a book it is unsound artistically on account of the balance disturbed by loving." She says she could rectify it but " ... that's how it *was.*"

The implication is that the teacher is a whole person and that anything that happens to that person affects that person's life as a teacher. Love may be upsetting but it can be enriching, and thereby enriches the life of the teacher.

All this is very honest and, in my view, courageous. But she nevertheless baulks at allowing the readers to know that the friendship was with another woman. So she quite simply turned Joy into a man—Saul. She must have thought that New Zealand was not ready for passionate friendships between women. She may well have been right. Apart from that one ... well ... deception, *Myself* rings true. It is one of my favourite books.

I do appear in a number of her books: *Incense to Idols* (1960), *Three* (1970), *I Passed This Way* (1980), and *Myself* (1967). I probably prefer the portrait of myself—yes, my own self, in *Myself*. I am Francis (or Frannie). She says: "He's the one who talks to himself, his imagination seeming to take charge completely. He has this way of looking upward and away from his surroundings so that one learns to expect from this far-off look some fairy tale. When K has lost something and asks Francis where it is, his fabrications are incredible."

Sylvia 5

Pipiriki was the crucible, the testing ground, where her ideas and direction began to take root. I use the word "direction" loosely, since it was never clear what this was. There were a number of conflicts: work/family; husband/loving friendships; teaching/writing; good person/bad person; and the biggest conflict of all: feeling/reason.

I'll start with the feeling/reason conflict, which she mentions in the introduction to *Myself*. It was probably a conflict which she never resolved but it certainly emerged in Pipiriki as a powerful theme in her life. We know that she was a passionate person capable of strong feeling—probably stronger than most. But does the strength of a feeling justify it, validate it? Because you feel something strongly, does it make it right?

Sylvia consulted the philosophers to try to find a solution to dilemmas. She read a lot of Bertrand Russell and Adler. But even though the wise ones provided the answers, she couldn't apply them to herself. She probably decided to become her own philosopher.

Sylvia had great difficulty making up her mind. She says in *I Passed This Way* that Elliot and Ashton couldn't stand it. She explained it to me once, saying that, as an artist, she could always see all sides of the question. Even when she chose a course of action she would soon find good reasons for abandoning it.

There is a more fanciful explanation in *I Passed This Way*. She was born a left-hander but her mother tied her left hand behind her back and forced her to use her right hand. Consequently she could use both hands to paint. Perhaps this had an effect on her mind, making her see both sides of every question. As with all the other conflicts in her life, Pipiriki seems to have given them a peculiar force and clarity. She does say somewhere that the topography and the forest and the river give a dangerously exaggerated power to them.

On the teaching/writing conflict she does say how much she hates teaching. But she never says she hates writing.

Sylvia 6

After the lush forests and the moody, winding river, and the turbulent emotions of Pipiriki, Waiomatatini, with its flat dry landscape, must have seemed a little bleak. In retrospect, Pipiriki looked like a paradise, but even paradises have their sell-by date. I had no sense of any general grief that we were leaving there. Three or four years were the maximum useful time to stay in one place. We adjusted fairly quickly.

Ashton and I had close Māori friends. Ashton was good mates with Tooti and I with Ben Ngata. Ben told me at Sylvia's funeral that we used to ride horses together across the plains. I remember on one occasion when we would gallop the horses, barebacked, across the riverbed and throw ourselves off the horse in full flight into a welcoming mud pool.

I discovered love in Waiomatatini. First there was Kino—a striking young Māori girl, with, I think, red hair. I painted a boat on a flat stone from the riverbed and gave it to her. She kept it for about three days and then threw it back at me from the other side of the classroom. The reason for this perplexed me then, and perplexes me still. Come in from the cold, Kino. I still love you.

Sylvia 7

The Waiomatatini River was a spectacularly changeable feature. In the summer, we would swim in the placid clear pools alongside the very small stream. In the winter it became, after the rains, a vast, lawless and terrifying torrent. It had its own taniwha which collected an annual tribute—that is, someone drowned every year. But if there was no one drowned in one year, the taniwha would take two the next. The nearest shop was across the river in Tikitiki. In the wet season the Māori men would swim their horses across. I would watch, aghast at the danger and their seeming lack of fear.

Sylvia was always quite good in a crisis. She could remain calm and take sensible measures to get through it. The weeping and the tantrums could be spectacularly summoned up if it was her own crisis. There were lots of these in Waiomataini. There would be a huge row at the back door between Keith and Sylvia before Sylvia would take off, crying, to Selah across the paddock.

In retrospect, I am not sure what these rows were about. It may have been Sylvia's isolation, the feeling that she had been dragged out of sight of civilisation and that Keith was to blame for this—or so, perhaps, she saw it. It was probably also a personality clash. But when they had a row, it produced its own momentum and tended to grow—organically, as it were, of its own accord—so that later it was impossible to remember how it started—a bit like the First World War, and the Second too, for that matter.

The school was run in an ordered fashion by Keith, who showed his usual indulgence towards Sylvia's erratic teaching schedule and, not least, her erratic appearances. But discipline was strong, based on the strap. There was a huge respect for Keith, not just for the school, but for the way it was integrated into the community. Māori culture was introduced in the syllabus. Māori action songs were splendidly developed. There were sporting visits and trips. The school was a huge part of the community, sustaining it and giving it direction. When we left, the tears were uncontrollable, on both sides.

Sylvia and Keith were very good friends with John and Leslie Shaw, who liked Sylvia a lot, precisely because of her aberrant behaviour. They recognised the lawless and amoral artist in her and clearly enjoyed her company. Keith and Sylvia loved the Shaws—as did we, the children. John Shaw was tall, funny and thoughtful and played spectacular boogie-woogie. Leslie was a wondrously effervescent, funny and beautiful woman. Perhaps the behaviour of none of them went down too well with the rock-hard morality of the time.

Sylvia 8

Waiomatatini may have been isolated but we weren't confined in our isolation. We went off on camping trips around the North Island. The trips were a great joy. I remember that we spent weeks on the riverbed outside Gisborne—a marvellously enjoyable time. Keith and Sylvia bought a trailer and tents, which we loaded up behind the old Ford V8 which Keith had acquired from somewhere. Once we went to Lake Waikaremoana where K and S took a summer job looking after the hotel and camping ground. Again these were memorable and enjoyable times, probably less so for Sylvia in the laundry room. But she took time out to play the piano in the lounge, where her presence and the quality of her playing inspired speculative comments from foreign visitors.

There is no doubt that the Ashton-Warner family was a flamboyant species—a vivacious and inventive tribe who were all fiercely proud to belong to it. Merely belonging to this tribe provided a ready-made excuse for exaggerated and eccentric behaviour. It was a badge of honour to create a wildly unlikely scenario which would grow and develop as it swept around the family in its various retellings.

I went to Blenheim once to see a cousin Marjorie. We talked about some of the more bizarre episodes in the family history. Her husband, who had married into this family, looked wistfully into the middle distance and said, "They were a very strange flock."

Sylvia 9

And so to Fernhill. Ashton and I were coming up to high school age, which made the move necessary. The high school was a mere six miles away by school bus. I had the last part of the year with Keith and started the next year, 1949, at Hastings High School, an exciting place to be. Overseas, the world was in ruins and we were sending food parcels to Britain. And yet our own lives were blessed with sunshine, a good education, sports like tennis, plenty of food, plenty to drink, wonderful girls and weekend work with time off on the splendid beaches.

Sylvia 10

In Fernhill School, Sylvia was thinking through the ways and means of using Māori culture to bring out the best in the children in the infant room. Since there were no suitable books in the Pākehā culture (if such a thing exists) it became clear that she would have to make her own. Out of this aspiration came the Ihaka books. They became central to her concept of what was the best way to get the children reading. It appears that the Department of Education acquired them, studied them, and subsequently lost them. Lynley Hood has looked at this question—and has come to no conclusion. It may be that there were several sets of books—and if they were lost, which ones were they? In retrospect it is impossible to find a path through the thickets of invention and wishful thinking—on both sides. Whatever the truth was, it is lost in the misty fields of claims and counter-claims.

In any case the Janet and John books were unsuitable, not just for Māori children, but also for Pākehā children. Sooner or later someone would have to denounce the imposition of middle-class English culture on the inhabitants of a distant colony. Sylvia's way of doing it would necessarily ruffle a few feathers.

At the same time as she was engaged in fine-tuning her own concepts of the infant room, Sylvia was writing a novel, which emerged later as *Spinster*. There was an occasion when the cast of *The Pirates of Penzance*, rehearsing with Miss Miller, came to Fernhill for a party. Ben Hawthorne, the best Major-General ever (and I have seen a few) tells the story of how Sylvia was talking to him and said, conspiratorially, "I'm writing a novel, you know."

Sylvia 11

Patterns of life established themselves early on in Fernhill. Ashton and I were at high school, Sylvia and Keith were fully engaged with Fernhill School. Sylvia had also commandeered the shed at the back of the school house, which became her Selah. She spent a lot of time out there, presumably working on *Spinster*. After our evening meal Keith would say to Sylvia, "We'll sort out the dishes. You go and do your work." He always made sure that she had time to do her work. Keith often comes across as a bit of a traditionalist, which in some ways he was. But, looking at it from another angle, you could say that he was a very modern husband, given his persistent encouragement of his wife's work.

Keith was a Freemason, a member of Rotary and voted National (i.e., centre right). I used to argue with him on world affairs. I would point out to him the noxious effect of American influence in the world. He replied, "It's just as well that the Americans are there to stop the Russians rampaging all over the place." Sylvia would talk in disparaging tones about the "almighty American dollar". She would speak of the Russians without the same contempt that she reserved for the Americans. On the other hand she would claim that she always saw both sides of every question.

Friday night was shopping night, when Sylvia and Keith went into Hastings and did the shopping for the week. They were both dedicated readers, so a visit to the library on a Friday night was *de rigueur*. They would return with piles of books, all of which they would read during the week. The themes of these books were often discussed at the dinner table. Keith, who was reading a biography of Victor Hugo, pointed out that the Frenchman was married and lived with his wife, but kept a mistress down the road for at least 20 years while he was in exile on the island of Jersey. I couldn't make up my mind whether I approved of this or not. But it did seem that the French had a somewhat relaxed attitude to the issues of love and marriage. I decided that I would have to explore this question more fully at a later stage—preferably in France. My wish to escape to France began when I was about 8 years old. There had to be something other than civilisation as defined by New Zealand.

Keith read a biography of Oscar Wilde, which he undoubtedly hugely enjoyed. He told us, again at the dinner table, that Oscar Wilde said: "When Americans get married they go to Niagara Falls for their honeymoon. But it is always a disappointment—the first of many in their marriages." There were other epigrams of the great man, but this was the one that stuck in my mind. Looking back on it, given the Wilde and Hugo stories, it is almost as if Keith were gently mocking his doomed attachment to his own marriage. My sister, Jasmine, once said, talking of a future husband, "I would sooner have hell with him than heaven with anyone else."

Perhaps there was something of that in Keith's feelings about his marriage, in that life without Sylvia would have been intolerable and worthless. The agony without her would have been greater than the torment within the marriage. I always thought that he had made a calculated decision to tough it out, come what may.

Sylvia 12

Fernhill was a new place, which meant that, for Sylvia, there would be new loves. These were not long in emerging, in the form of Charlie Panckhurst and the Reverend Carr. Charlie was a young teacher from Hastings who appeared from nowhere and often turned up at the house. We liked him. We had no reason not to. He was a handsome, engaging young man who clearly enjoyed spending time with Sylvia. He had a good singing voice and sang operatic arias with Sylvia at the piano. As usual the relationship was much more intense for Sylvia than it was for Charlie. Later on he confessed to being quite fond of Sylvia, but no more than that. I recall him coming round to the house. In fact he sold me his bicycle for £10, which I thought was a pretty good deal. Sylvia did say later that she thought I had ripped him off. If I did, I am very sorry and do indeed apologise to Charlie, if he's still around.

And there was the Reverend Carr, a minister in a church in Hastings. I recall him well as a gentle, thoughtful man. Apparently he leaned into the car Sylvia was driving and kissed her. This caused Sylvia to be swept away by another frenzy of passion. She even told Keith that about the kiss, which prompted his comment: "I'll knock his block off!" I heard him say it. This response of Keith would seem to indicate that he was not entirely indifferent to Sylvia's carry-ons.

I was sitting with Keith in the sitting room one night. He looked grave and grey. He said, "She should have married John. I feel like a millstone round her neck." That must have been John Barron, one of her earlier, more flamboyant suitors.

The Reverend Carr prompted Sylvia to take a much greater than usual interest in his church. She was a regular during his sermons on Sunday evening, arriving flamboyantly at the last minute and sitting up the front, and then leaving regally and majestically right after the service. The church later became the setting for her novel *Incense to Idols*.

In the meantime Ashton and I had our high school years. I did my final year in the Upper Sixth, still doing Latin and French. There were just two of us left, Denis Goldman and myself. Mr Mathieson introduced us to the *Odes* of Horace, which I thought were just about the most amazing creations ever. As indeed did Horace himself, who claimed, quite justly, I thought, they would outlast the pyramids. I used to learn them off by heart and recite them to myself on the bus from Fernhill to Hastings.

Sylvia 13

We got through High School somehow, in spite of a few troublesome escapades. I was accredited with University Entrance which was one of the happiest days of my life. Armed with this I went off to Wellington. Ashton was there as well, working towards his certificates. For a time we both lived in a hostel in Oriental Bay. I got a job in the Public Trust which allowed time off to go up the hill to attend lectures at the university. Ashton and I came back regularly to Fernhill for the weekend. We were drawn back to Sylvia and Keith because we liked to see them and enjoyed telling them about our adventures in the big, wild world. It has to be said, though, that we had different sets of friends in Wellington.

Keith and Sylvia remained in Fernhill until about 1958 when they went to Bethlehem School just outside Tauranga. I left the Public Trust and went full-time to university, which I financed by summer work in Hawke's Bay. There was the Birds Eye factory, or the freezing works, or driving a truck.

Sylvia 14

My departure for university spelled the end of my childhood and youth with Sylvia and Keith. I spent five happy years at university. We were taught by the best minds in New Zealand. My greatest excitement was probably my discovery of French literature and particularly the French poets, notably Charles Baudelaire, whose poems I have kept within reach all my life.

Spinster came out in 1958, while I was at university. It created a huge impact. I achieved a certain mild notoriety when friends found out that I was the author's son. It was a role I enjoyed, since it gave me a little proxy fame.

One day James K. Baxter, the poet, came into the cafeteria carrying *Spinster,* and sat at my table with a few others. *Spinster* had received rave reviews in *Time* magazine. Baxter addressed the table, in his regal manner from his own pulpit: "A review in *Time* magazine is neither here nor there. Depends on whether it's a good book or not. I think it is a very fine book."

The oracle had spoken. I was fascinated by the whiff of smugness in Baxter's attitude. I thought that to get a good review in *Time* magazine was pretty good. The intelligentsia in New Zealand were divided, notably Joan Stevens, who didn't like its raw feeling. *Time* magazine said that Miss Ashton-Warner had been "roasted with chauvinistic prejudice by her own countrymen". The stage was set for Sylvia's difficult subsequent relationship with her fellow citizens, if this had not already been firmly established.

Sylvia 15

In December 1962, I left New Zealand, after two years teaching in Wellington. I spent four or five years in France, mainly in Paris. During this time, *Incense to Idols*, arguably one of the best of Sylvia's novels, was published. I then returned to London where I landed a good job in a university institute. There was a marriage, my son Vincent was born, and then Keith became terminally ill. I returned to New Zealand in 1970 and saw Keith briefly before he died.

When I returned to London, via Mauritius, I became seriously ill with a tropical disease. Jacquemine, my wife, having escaped to Mauritius, returned. Sylvia came to London to offer support, as did Ashton, who saved my life with his strong presence. I eventually emerged from hospital and lived in my flat with Sylvia, Jacquemine, and an actor friend, Graeme Eton. Graeme was valuable for lifting heavy things, which I couldn't do. It became clear that Jacquemine and Sylvia didn't get on. There was the implication from Sylvia that Jacquemine's lackadaisical ways were responsible for my illness. It may be that drinking unfiltered water in Mauritius had something to do with it.

From this time came the novel *Three*. I still find it painful to read, but I would not have wanted to prevent its publication, even though I do not come out of it very well. Everyone has a right to publish whatever they want, in my view.

During the time I lived in London I received regular letters from Sylvia, all of which I have kept. After she died, I collected them all and put them into a bank vault, having taken copies of them. They will be safe in a library one day. I also wrote letters to Sylvia (as well as to Jasmine, my sister, and Ashton). My letters to Sylvia are now in the Alexander Turnbull Library in Wellington. So there is a good record of all our lives.

I visited Sylvia regularly and even went to see her in Vancouver. It was there that I met the head of department of her faculty at

Simon Fraser University. We talked about Sylvia and her work in the department. He ran his hand over his brow and said that he had had a lot of trouble getting her co-operation. I responded by saying: "My mother is the most difficult woman in the world."

He reported this to Sylvia who included the comment in *I Passed This Way*. When I went to receive her prize from the Alpha Omega Society in the United States, I told this story to the 2,000 women in the Renaissance Centre in Chicago. They loved it. It certainly helped sales. I sold about 500 copies after my speech.

Jasmine and I spent the last month with Sylvia and were with her when she died. There were signs that she was fearful of the judgement of Jesus Christ. When she took her last breath I stood there, awestruck that this vital force had been finally stilled. But I felt, too, that death was part of some cycle that we didn't understand. After her cremation, in accordance with her request, we scattered her ashes over Tauranga Harbour. Later on Bill, Jasmine's husband, with determined persistence, included her name on Keith's grave, so that they were together in spirit. The citation concludes: "To the children of the world."

References

Ashton-Warner, S. (1958). *Spinster*. London: Secker & Warburg.

Ashton-Warner, S. (1960). *Incense to idols*. London: Secker & Warburg.

Ashton-Warner, S. (1967). *Myself*. New York: Simon & Schuster.

Ashton-Warner, S. (1970). *Three*. New York: Knopf.

Ashton-Warner, S. (1980). *I passed this way*. Wellington: A. H & A. W. Reed.

Author

Elliot Henderson is the elder son of Sylvia Ashton-Warner and her husband Keith Henderson. He spent his early years at various schools in New Zealand where Keith and Sylvia were headmaster and infant mistress. He received his secondary education at Hastings High School and went on from there to study French and English at Victoria University of Wellington. He continued his French studies at the University of Paris, and was appointed Senior Lecturer in French at one of the university institutes in London. He spends most of his time in London, pursuing his interests in literature and music, but makes regular visits to New Zealand.
Email: elliotkh@hotmail.com

CHAPTER 11

Who is Sylvia? The story of a biography

Lynley Hood

New Zealander Lynley Hood published her award-winning biography *Sylvia!* in 1988, and the diary of her research process (Who is Sylvia?) in 1990. Here Hood recalls the process of writing about a woman who was, to everyone who knew her, an enigma.[1]

---

1   This chapter is based on Lynley Hood's book *Who is Sylvia?* (1990).

Revisiting Sylvia Ashton-Warner has taken me back 25 years—to my decision to write my first book (Hood, 1988). I was not—and am not now—a teacher, or a journalist, or a scholar of New Zealand literature. I was, and still am, a scientist by training and a freelance writer by occupation. I was fascinated by Sylvia Ashton-Warner because she was a controversial figure, and high-profile controversies have always fascinated me. Both parties can't be right, so where does the truth lie? For writers of my ilk, high-profile controversies are magnifying glasses through which we may bring into sharper focus matters that in the normal course of events remain blurry—matters of love and hate, of fact and fiction, of memory and forgetting, and of human nature itself. About 25 years ago, in August 1983, I wrote to Sylvia (see Hood, 1990, p. 12):

12 August 1983

Dear Mrs Henderson

I had the pleasure of reading your autobiography late last year and was stimulated by it to re-read your earlier books.

Many of the themes in your writing—love, creativity, passion—strike a rich chord within me. As a mother I have great respect for your contribution to early childhood education. But there is much about you and your life that puzzles me.

For all these reasons I am fired with a single-minded ambition; I want to write your biography.

As far as I have been able to find out no biography of Sylvia Ashton-Warner has been written. I feel there is a great need for one so that the public may better appreciate your contribution to education.

If you are interested in this proposal I would very much like to come to Tauranga and discuss it with you further.

As for myself—I am a Dunedin freelance writer, married with three children. I write mainly on parenting, health and current affairs and have had my work published in the *Listener*, the *NZ Woman's Weekly* and the *NZ Medical Journal* as well as in daily papers. I have also written health education booklets and workbooks for the Heart Foundation and the Otago Hospital Board.

I look forward to your reply,

Lynley Hood

At the time, Sylvia was living a reclusive life in Tauranga and rarely answered letters from strangers, but she answered mine (Hood, 1990, p. 13):

Aug 23, 83

Dear Lynley Hood: thanks for your letter. You must be brave to take on someone's biography. I've said No three times so far but I think it will be Yes this time.

Everyone's complex ... I think I am. I'm very seventy-four now and may not make an easy subject. On the other hand you might make it fun.

It would need to be this year as we do grow old, though there is much that is pleasant ... aging.

Yes it would be worth it ... coming to Tauranga ... but then I think of the expense it would be for you, and what about the children? I suppose they're lovely. What are their names?

With best wishes. I enjoyed your letter.

S. Henderson
(Ashton-Warner)

I visited Sylvia in October 1983 and found a very wrinkled, very forceful old lady who seemed to have made up her mind, even before we met, that I was going to write her biography. Her grand-daughter, Corinne, was with us on that first day, and after we'd been talking for about an hour said, "Grandma, I've never heard you being so open with anybody! You're usually so guarded."

"Lynley's asking all the right questions," Sylvia said. "Every one hits the mark."

I made two more visits to her at the end of 1983, staying for two or three days each time. And I saw her again early in 1984, just before she died.

Researching Sylvia

In the course of researching the book, I interviewed hundreds of people who had some connection with Sylvia's life and work. I tape-recorded most interviews, but if my subject was anxious about being taped I just took notes. And if note taking made them nervous I just listened—and made notes immediately afterwards. My overriding concern was to get the story right, rather than to get it verbatim.

My interviewees included Sylvia herself, her surviving brother and sister, her children, scores of friends, relatives, teachers, writers, education officials, acquaintances and pupils. I wasn't just looking for descriptions of events. In an effort to understand the emotional reality of Sylvia's life, I also asked about thoughts and feelings. And in an effort to understand the texture and colour of her life I sought detail—gestures, mannerisms, clothing, decor and so on.

Meeting the people who appeared as thinly disguised characters in Sylvia's novels always seemed a bit unreal—the word made flesh, as it were. I spent years chasing a trail littered with wild geese and red herrings before I tracked down Charles Panckhurst—the model for Paul in *Spinster*. I discovered along the way that he did not in fact splatter himself over the ceiling as Paul did in *Spinster*, or depart for England, as he did in Sylvia's diary.

I arrived at his Whakatāne school at 3 o'clock one afternoon, thinking "Is this really happening—am I really going to meet Paul from *Spinster*?" When I asked directions to Charles Panckhurst's room I half expected the school secretary to fall about laughing and say "Don't be silly, he's just a character in a novel," but she directed me to a prefab in the middle of the playground. Then the bell rang, the prefab door flew open and dozens of little Māori children came pouring out. I felt as if I'd walked straight onto the set of *Spinster*.

I tracked down some people in the most unexpected ways. Wellesley Aron was the man who had invited Sylvia to help set up a peace school in Israel. I knew almost nothing about him. For all I knew he could be dead. And if he was still alive I had no way of finding him. I was mulling over this problem one evening when the religious programme came on the radio. I was about to switch it off when I heard something about Israel ... Peace school ... Wellesley Aron ... and then ... the voice of the man himself. As Sylvia said of Ngaio Marsh's radio review of *Spinster*, "I could hardly hear for listening!" I took down the name of the school and wrote to the Israeli embassy for the address. Then I wrote to Wellesley Aron and a short time later received a tape of reminiscences and a sheaf of photocopied correspondence. And so another lead was successfully run to ground.

Former pupils

When I came to talk with Sylvia's former pupils I wondered whether they would repeat to me the episodes that Sylvia wrote about in *Spinster* and *Teacher*, but this never happened.

In *Teacher*, Sylvia deplored the imposition of reading material from the alien culture onto the tender minds of her Māori 5-year-olds, but, according to her pupils, in most classroom activities the imposition of the alien culture was all-important. Sylvia spent hours playing Schubert, Brahms, and above all, Beethoven's Fifth, on the classroom piano.

One day at Fernhill School she brought a touring concert pianist to visit her infant room. He asked the children what they'd like him to play—of course, he was expecting requests for things like "Twinkle, twinkle, little star", but one barefoot little lad from the pā piped up, "Would you play the one that goes—Da Da Da DUM!"

Sylvia's concerts were legendary. They featured items like "The Wedding of the Painted Doll", "The Pied Piper", "Hiawatha", "Old Mother Hubbard", and never a Māori topic to be seen.

None of her former pupils spontaneously mentioned reading lessons, so eventually I would feel constrained to ask, "Do you remember being taught to read?" The answer was usually, "No." So I'd prompt: "Do you remember her giving you cards with words on?" That did strike a chord with one guy. He said, "Yees … Yees … she was always doing that … I don't know what that was about. Do you know what that was about?" What could I say? The technique for which she was world-famous. The technique that was supposed to make everything clear. It was still a mystery to that particular pupil. I mentioned this apparent amnesia to Dawn Percy, an art advisor who had spent time in Sylvia's classroom. She said, "No, they wouldn't remember. The reading lessons were so much a part of their lives. Reading and writing was as natural to those kids as breathing."

I did eventually meet some former pupils from Sylvia's 1951 class at Fernhill, and they had colourful tales to tell. And this is an important point: the events Sylvia wrote about in *Teacher* took place at Fernhill School in 1951. She discovered the key vocabulary, she wrote up her teaching scheme, and she made little reading books based on her pupils' own lives in 1951. She did not do these things before 1951. And after 1951 she spent more and more time in Selah and less and less time at school. People who knew Sylvia at Horoera or Pipiriki or Waiomatatini or Bethlehem or Aspen or Vancouver can tell us a lot about Sylvia and her work, but only the people who were in her classroom in 1951 can tell us about Sylvia's use of the key vocabulary with Māori 5-year-olds.

One such 5-year-old was Pere Hanara, and his memories were vivid (see Hood, 1988, pp. 136–137).

> One day Gilbert Nuku threw a ball inside and broke the window. He was sent to get the strap and when he came back Mrs Henderson gave

him the words *ball*, *window* and *glass*, and made him write them down. He learnt them. Gilbert was a bit of a dunce but when it came to the word "window", he knew it. After school when we went home and played marbles in the dirt we used to talk about our words. "I know a bigger word than you—what's your word?"

"My word's *jalopy*."

And Gilbert used to say, "My word is *window*."

I thought—Gee, Gilbert got a big word. I wonder what word I could learn next?

But when it came to Sylvia's reading books, Pere was less than impressed: "Actually, I liked Janet and John better."

Memories and versions

One of the recurring problems with my research was that I would get several different versions of the same event. Which one should I believe? With one episode in Sylvia's life, I received three different versions and I put all three in the biography. With other episodes I weighed the evidence and came down in favour of one version rather than another. In evaluating such stories, I began by assuming that accounts written at the time of the event were probably more reliable than memories of the same event recalled 30 years later, but I discovered this isn't always the case.

The writer Noel Hilliard told me about the evening Keith Henderson invited him and some others to the Henderson home in Bethlehem for a meal. While the guests were sitting around talking, Sylvia took a roast out of the oven and put it on top of the piano. Then she sat down and began playing. Noel said she just sat there playing for hours while the meat got cold and the potatoes boiled away to a pulp. I said, "So you had cold meat and pulpy potatoes?" He said, "No! We never ate. We just sat there getting hungrier and hungrier while she went on playing the bloody piano." Noel hunted out his diary to see what he'd written at the time. And what he had written was something like—"spent the evening with Sylvia and Keith Henderson"—that was all. However I was able to confirm Noel's story with Hone Tuwhare and others who were there that night.

I think the fact that Noel couldn't bring himself to write about that bizarre episode at the time is interesting. It may have something to do with the storytelling process. When we tell a story, or write it down, there's a logical sequence of words, the story has a beginning, a middle and an end—and the whole thing makes some kind of sense.

But the roast-on-top-of-the-piano story makes no sense at all. It takes time for our minds to turn this sort of mind-boggling strangeness into a logical sequence of words.

People sometimes get their facts wrong. Greg Tata is a case in point. Greg was taught by Sylvia at Bethlehem School. Later, he travelled the world as a musician and teacher. Whenever he returned to Tauranga he had coffee with Sylvia and they reminisced about Keith Henderson, Bethlehem School and their overseas travels. Greg told me that he bumped into Sylvia in Piccadilly Circus around 1969. This was quite possible. Sylvia was in London at that time. He also claimed to have run into her in the New Zealand Consulate in New York, whereupon they went to a Lebanese restaurant and reminisced about Keith Henderson and Bethlehem School. I searched Sylvia's diaries and letters and cross-examined her acquaintances, and I can tell you with absolute certainty that Sylvia has never been to New York—but she could have run into Greg at the New Zealand Consulate in San Francisco or Vancouver, and they may have gone for a Lebanese meal … who knows?

Greg also claimed to have run into Sylvia in the Champs-Élysées in Paris, where they had a cup of coffee and reminisced about Keith Henderson and Bethlehem School. Once again, I checked Sylvia's diaries and letters. I cross-examined her acquaintances, and I checked her passport. And I can tell you with absolute certainty that Sylvia has never set foot in France. I can only conclude that Sylvia convinced Greg over coffee in Tauranga that those overseas meetings really did happen. This would be quite within Sylvia's power.

In Aspen, she convinced four highly intelligent, well-educated, normally rational people, in the teeth of a great deal of evidence to the contrary, that her life was in danger and they had to spirit her away in the dead of night. The fact that they did so without question bears witness to Sylvia's extraordinary charisma.

Nuggets

My research took me to places as well as people. I visited all the places in New Zealand where Sylvia lived and worked. I went to Aspen, Vancouver and London where she lived overseas. I visited her publishers in London, New York and Auckland, and her archives in Boston. And I went all over the United States, and to Paris, to meet people who featured in her life.

Searching through Sylvia's archives was like panning for gold. From time to time I came across glints of precious metal and even, occasionally, a real nugget, but I had to sift through mountains of dross along the way. I'm sure Sylvia gained some amusement from sending guarantees for household appliances to her archive in the Mugar Memorial Library at Boston University, but that's not the sort of thing biographers are really interested in.

Among the nuggets were examples of one of Sylvia's most appealing qualities—her marvellously whimsical sense of humour. This is a letter she wrote to the Dean Martin Sullivan, to thank him for his radio review of *Spinster*. Like most of us when faced with the clergy, she started out to show what a nice person she was. But she soon realised the absurdity of it all and went over the top in sending herself up. She finishes the letter with

> I hope you will come and see Mr Henderson and me some time. We are remarkably nice people. We're courteous and gentle and are always

making coffee or tea. We often answer the phone when it rings and have been known to return calls. Social calls. We can prove it. We go carefully to church. Keith because he likes the singing and I because I like the level of argument from the pulpit. I write the most gracious letters refusing to talk to clubs and bodies and give personal interviews and Keith most generously promises to buy me some stockings or a new handbag with my royalties. We're known to be very-nicely-dressed, very-nicely-spoken and very-nicely-behaved people. I can recommend that you come and see us. There's always ENOUGH beds, although I did back the car into the spare one in the garage the other day. We always back the car into the garage in preparation for driving out with dignity, the next time.

Thank you for your review. I put aside the effort of trying to believe the position you accorded me in New Zealand letters.

Sylvia Henderson

(Hood, 1990, p. 274)

But underneath the wit and the whimsy was a complex and often unhappy woman. She sometimes wrote revealing letters, but these were never posted. Instead, Sylvia sealed each one in its own stamped, addressed envelope and placed it in a red box. One of the highlights of my research was of sitting down with that red box in the Mugar Memorial Library and methodically slitting open and reading each letter. Several unposted letters were to Dunedin psychiatrist Harold Bourne.

Dear Dr Bourne

There is already a fine, thoughtful letter, hand-posted in my unposted letter box to Doctor Bourne, thanking him for the time and care he put into his talk on "Why people write novels", which would have been posted in the letter-box in town but for the fact that it was honest and sincere.

Later: I was called to the phone by my bookseller who said I was to sign the New York contract. This disturbed me so much that I put a batch of wholemeal scones in the oven to compose myself. Then Mr Henderson came home for lunch and we went all American and Dollar-y for an hour. Then to organise my thinking enough to write to New York and to finish your letter I weeded my long thin flower bed in a high wind. The weeds in question have a long thin white root that reaches down into the garden's unconscious to a dynamic little bulb which, if you do not remove it, only grows again. I wish the garden could utterly relax to allow these hidden bulbs to come up of their own accord as our own hidden impulses do with that treatment. I wouldn't want my mind to be as rigid and resisting and unco-operating as my garden, nor my most heavily covered thoughts to be as inaccessible as the bulbs of the weeds. Nor would I like to think that my behaviour is such a mass of symptoms as the surface of my garden is a mass of foliage. What my garden should do is write a book and clean up the underground mess.

Thank you for your able discussion of "Why people write novels." I'd like to hear you speak now on "Why people can't write anymore." With emphasis on the posthumous state. With attention to rhythm and nervous energy. "With work and fevers over." Have you got among your equipment a direction-finder? Does it point to weeding the garden, making scones or heading back into the furnace of writing.

And so on. What is your fee? I'll post it.

Sincerely

Sylvia Henderson

(Hood, 1990, p. 275)

What does it all mean?

In writing the book, I had to take the gold extracted from 35 manuscript boxes, 20 cartons, several filing cabinets of documents, one tea chest of photographs, and four shoe boxes of tape recordings—and shape it into a life. I didn't want to write a biography that was just a recital of facts, so the overriding question was: What does it all mean? When I turned to people who had an interest in Sylvia, I found most of them grouped into hostile armies on either side of a vast abyss. To some people, Sylvia was a saint and a martyr; to others, she was a fraud and a poseur. She was also, undoubtedly, a mass of contradictions and a woman who refused to be pigeonholed, or understood.

One day I drew a line down a piece of paper and listed on one side the qualities that attracted people to her, and on the other side the qualities that drove people away. To my astonishment, I ended up with two identical lists. The reason for this is that people responded differently to Sylvia, depending on who they were and the context of the interaction. If you were an official of any sort, I can guarantee that Sylvia would have driven you up the wall. The way she approached life on her own terms, and the wildly original way in which her mind worked, enchanted her fans and made her the uniquely creative person she was, but it also made her an administrator's nightmare. This is a letter to Bob Gottlieb explaining why she couldn't go on a publicity tour. After thanking him for the invitation, she wrote

> I am however a notorious guest. I cannot catch anything that leaves anywhere at a certain time, I think of something else when someone is talking earnestly to me, then I don't know what to answer, or answer something he asked a half hour ago, or even yesterday.
>
> I forget names immediately I am told, and if I have an appointment I sort of crumble, then dissolve, then kind of melt and drain away in little streams of nothing and stay like that until the appointment time is over; only to reassemble immediately and make the tea.[2]

Among the people who didn't have a lot of time for Sylvia were the more traditionally minded teachers and inspectors in the Māori school service (but there were also many teachers and inspectors who liked and admired her a lot). It's not that Sylvia's critics were horrible, narrow-minded people—though no doubt some of them were; the majority were decent New Zealanders who knew right from wrong

---

2   From the author's personal collection of copies of letters between Robert Gottlieb and Sylvia Ashton-Warner. This letter is undated, from the 1960s.

and who didn't believe in rocking the boat. Sylvia upset them because she was eccentric and flamboyant and recklessly nonconforming at a time when showing off was one of the seven deadly sins. Also, she was pursuing a career as a writer at a time when women were supposed to know their place, and their place was in the kitchen. The role reversal in the Henderson household in the 1930s, '40s and '50s was a considerable threat to the status quo.

One of Sylvia's qualities that made life particularly difficult for the people around her was that, as a writer, she was turning life into fiction at the same time she was living it. She tended to live by the scenario she was working out in her head, and since the people around her hadn't read the script they could never figure out what the hell was going on. Also, every good story needs lots of drama. So in the interests of her art, Sylvia never hesitated to bring any simmering pot around her to a very vigorous boil.

When *Spinster* came out in 1958, what really got up the noses of education officials was that the heroine claimed to be a lone voice in a sea of reactionary indifference, when in reality the events in *Spinster* took place at a time when the move to child-centred education was in full flood and the famous "play-way" debate was at its most vociferous.

The other problem was that Sylvia presented herself, through her heroine in *Spinster* and through her own voice in *Teacher*, as a truly dedicated teacher, when it was common knowledge that she never marked the roll, never kept a workbook and never did playground duty. Her school attendance was often irregular and her breath sometimes smelled of alcohol. The attitude of her critics could best be summed up by the education official who roared at me down the telephone, "Of course, you know she was a hopeless teacher, and mad as a meat axe." When I ran this comment past art advisor Dawn Percy she thought for a moment. Then she said, "Mad as a meat axe—yes. Hopeless teacher—no!!"

Sylvia's genius was that she transcended all this outer chaos and inner instability and wrote books that have enchanted readers and inspired thousands of teachers. When I ask fans of *Teacher* what it is about the book that so enthuses them, they say things like, "She affirmed something I knew deep down to be true, and she gave me the courage to translate those truths into action." Which may be another way of saying, "She enabled me to recognise and name my own key vocabulary."

In trying to make sense of Sylvia, her own words were my main source. She spoke and wrote of her need for creative self-expression, of her identification with Māori 5-year-olds and of her struggle with what she called "the dark forces of the undermind that determine our actions". Among those dark forces were her paradoxical cravings for unconditional love and admiration on the one hand, and for betrayal and rejection on the other. As poet Louis Johnson observed: "The truth of the matter probably is that Sylvia needed rejection more than she needed support—because that's what she fed on."

What to put in; what to leave out

Once a pattern began to emerge in the jigsaw puzzle, I started to write the book. One thing I really agonised over was what to put in and what to leave out. I focused on Sylvia's life—rather than on her contributions to literature and education—but even so I had a mountain of data to deal with. I didn't want to write a long book. I didn't want to include events just because they happened, or letters just because they were written, or comments just because they were said. I wanted everything I included to serve a purpose—to evoke a mood, to mark a milestone in Sylvia's life, to illuminate a scene or a character, to provide balance, or to move the story forward.

Anything trivial or repetitive was left out. But that created more problems. I had to look hard at everything I left out and say—is this really repetitive or irrelevant? Or am I leaving this out because it doesn't fit the picture I've built up of Sylvia Ashton-Warner? I was determined that if I came upon evidence that contradicted my understanding of her, then the understanding would have to be discarded—not the evidence.

The issue of how to handle the darker side of Sylvia, which was so different from the picture she presented of herself, was a painful one. There were many times when I wished she hadn't been so selfish or cruel, and if she had been, I wished I didn't have to write about it. I didn't want to do a hatchet job—but neither did I want to do a whitewash. I decided that her dark side had to go in because her life made no sense without it. Ultimately, my primary concern was not to reveal or conceal but simply to get the story right, and to write about it as fairly and accurately and sensitively as I could.

It was important to me that the biography be a good read. I wanted to not only reconstruct a life, but to breathe into it the warmth of a life being lived, and to this end I tried to write a book that read like a novel. Wherever possible I did things that novelists do—like using a scene-by-scene development, rather than a running narrative. Instead of long descriptive passages, I tried to weave the sights and sounds in and out of the action. I used detail to more vividly evoke the drama and passion of Sylvia's life, but, unlike a novelist, the details I used—the gestures, the comments, the clothes and so on—were researched rather than invented.

I also wanted to provoke the reader's imagination. When the dramatic scenes took place I wanted the reader to be there. But, of course, the details I gave them to work with were always researched, never invented. I allowed many of the characters to tell their own stories in their words by using lots of direct quotes. Direct quotes add authenticity to the text, they reveal personalities and they provide colourful variations to the cadence and rhythm of the prose.

I felt it was important not to over explain or over describe. I just wanted to throw out a few flares so that the reader would understand Sylvia by illumination, rather than explanation. And this is where vocabulary was important. I often used to think that it would have been much easier to explain Sylvia if I lived in an age that believed in witchcraft and demonic possession, and when it came to describing the effect she had on a group of academics and teachers who came to sit at her feet in Aspen, I found the language of witchcraft extremely useful

> During afternoons and evenings, they met with Sylvia over drinks and meals, and all day she held them spellbound with the vitality of her being, the warmth of her manner, and the poetry, mystery and wisdom of her words.
>
> They were so bewitched that even aspects of Sylvia's behaviour that would have concerned them in anyone else seemed no more than delightful eccentricities in such a wonderful woman: her claim that she was a five-year-old child entranced them, her talk of being on a "lager and lettuce diet" (if she drank more than six bottles of lager a day, as she usually did, she ate only lettuce the next day) charmed them, and the vast collection of brandy bottles in her coat cupboard (she said they were presents from *Spinster* fans, and that she never drank the stuff) enchanted them further. (Hood, 1988, p. 213)

So I haven't actually said the woman was a witch and that explains everything—but I have set the mood for the strange events that unfolded at Aspen by using words like *spellbound*, *bewitched*, *entranced*, *charmed* and *enchanted*.

I struggled to be true to Sylvia and true to everyone else in the story, and where anything sensitive was involved I consulted with the people concerned to make sure that I'd got it right. But I did not consult anyone about what I should put in, and what I should leave out. I was the author and such decisions were my responsibility. My primary concern was with the truth. Of course I'm not for a minute suggesting that there is only one truth, and that I have a monopoly on it, but there's a world of difference between telling the truth as I see it and suppressing or distorting the perceived facts in order to keep everyone happy.

This doesn't mean that questions of hurt or offence were not important—I gave them a lot of thought and many passages were drafted and redrafted with this in mind, but the bottom line was this: if an episode was crucial to the understanding of Sylvia—it had to go in.

The ghost of Sylvia

When I first met Sylvia's son Elliot, I noted in my diary that he seemed relieved to be passing on the torch of understanding his mother to me. Later there were times when the task seemed not so much a torch as a great suffocating burden. Sometimes I felt like Brave Orchid, in Maxine Hong Kingston's book *The Woman Warrior*. As a deliberate act of bravado, Brave Orchid spent the night in a haunted room. During the night, the ghost came and sat on her chest and almost suffocated her. When her friends found her in the morning she was close to death. They had to chant secret incantations to restore her spirit to her body.

One of the incantations I used to keep the ghost of Sylvia at bay was a mental list headed WAYS IN WHICH I AM NOT LIKE SYLVIA. The list was a very negative one. It included Sylvia's selfishness, arrogance, jealousy, hot-headedness, irrationality, snobbishness and so on. I'd probably been keeping it for a while before I even realised I was doing it. But when I caught myself reciting this list I thought, "Why am I doing this? Why is it so important for me to be not like Sylvia?" In a moment of raw honesty I realised that the negative qualities in Sylvia that I was so anxious to disown in fact belonged to me all along. The ghost I was fighting was really the dark side of myself. And having accepted those qualities in myself, I no longer find them anything like as objectionable in Sylvia. In fact I see things like selfishness and arrogance as essential qualities in any writer. They're certainly part and parcel of what I most admire in Sylvia—her reckless nonconformity, her commitment to the life of the spirit, the unassailability of her chosen positions in life, and her determination to be true to herself no matter what the cost.

Those four years I spent on Sylvia Ashton-Warner's biography were among the most challenging, extending and enjoyable years of my life. At the end of it I became like her in more ways than I care to think about. I've also inherited many of her friends and enemies—though some of the friends have become enemies, and some of the enemies have become friends. But, most importantly, those years transformed me from a sociable part-time scribbler to a solitary full-time writer—with all the changes of philosophy and lifestyle and self-image that such a transformation entails. In the course of writing the book I met a lot of people who said, "Knowing Sylvia Ashton-Warner changed my life." She certainly changed mine.

References

Hong Kingston, M. (1977). *The woman warrior: Memoirs of a girlhood among ghosts*. New York : Vintage Books.

Hood, L. (1988). *Sylvia! The biography of Sylvia Ashton-Warner*. Auckland: Viking

Hood, L. (1990). *Who is Sylvia? The diary of a biography*. Dunedin: John McIndoe

Author

Lynley Hood is a Dunedin-based scientist, independent scholar and writer. Her qualifications include an MSc in Physiology and a LittD for "published contributions of special excellence in literary, social and historical knowledge". She is the author of four books, a stage play and many book chapters and articles. Her books are: *Sylvia! The Biography of Sylvia Ashton-Warner; Who Is Sylvia? The Diary of a*

Biography of Sylvia Ashton-Warner; *Minnie Dean: Her Life and Crimes* (a biography of the only woman hanged for murder in New Zealand) and *A City Possessed: The Christchurch Civic Crèche Case: Child Abuse, Gender Politics & the Law*. Both *Sylvia*! and *A City Possessed* won New Zealand's premier nonfiction book awards.
Email: ljhood@ihug.co.nz

Index

activity methods 71, 122, 217
advisors 71
Allen, Dr Donald 13, 112
Alley
    Gwen 72
    Joy (also Somerset). 123, 181, 182
America/ U.S.A. 68, 105, 112, 130, 132
Art and/or crafts
    carving 70
    clay modelling 151, 163
    drawing 24, 24, 46, 47
    Māori arts and crafts 67, 70, 94
    murals 123
    painting 24, 46, 78, 151, 164
artist 8, 54, 59, 65, 76, 77, 78, 86, 87, 101, 103, 106, 110, 147, 156, 159, 164, 184, 186
Asia 105
Aspen, Colorado, U.S.A. 13, 202, 205, 212
autobiography 5, 7, 13, 60, 87, 96, 119, 123, 129, 139, 198

Ball, Douglas 67, 72
Barrington, J. 169
Beeby, C.E. 32, 71, 72, 121
Bell Call 7, 11, 79, 85, 87, 88, 92, 97, 103, 104, 105, 106, 107, 129
bilingualism 68, 79, 114

biography 6, 7, 8, 12, 14, 87, 90, 137, 189, 197, 198, 199, 203, 207, 211, 214, 215

Canada
    Simon Fraser University 11, 13, 113, 145, 146, 157, 159, 194
    Vancouver 13, 14, 140, 145, 146, 158, 159, 193, 202, 204, 205
church 42, 190, 191, 206
civilisation 68, 79, 185, 189
Clemens, Sydney Gurewitz 8, 9, 15, 62, 82
colonialism 168
correspondence 64, 120, 130, 132, 133, 139, 141, 201
creativity 33, 39, 52, 54, 55, 56, 59, 61, 74, 78, 114, 123, 198
cultural integration policy 70, 77
Curnow, Allen 89, 90, 109
curriculum 9, 63, 65, 66, 67, 69, 70, 73, 116, 154

dance 25, 28, 46, 48, 54, 59, 70, 123, 150, 158
    poi 70
democracy 65, 66
Department of Education 71, 120, 163, 175, 188

Depression 62, 65, 73
Dewey, John 65, 82, 122
discipline 21, 48, 62, 63, 78, 104, 186
Dog Rib 146, 147, 156

editors
    Bond, Russell 19, 116, 117, 118, 119, 120, 121, 122, 125
    Gottlieb, Robert 12, 13, 112, 121, 129, 142, 143, 208
    Lowry, Robert 115, 120
England/Britain 63, 89, 105, 124, 130, 139, 142, 187, 200
English language 162, 168
Europe 78
European 20, 22, 53, 64, 72, 79, 80, 93, 94, 98

Fernhill 13, 113, 114, 118, 125, 187, 188, 190, 191, 192, 201, 202
film
    Sylvia: 14, 15
    Two Loves 16
Fitt, Professor A. 67, 79
France/ French 9, 44, 64, 189, 191, 192, 193, 195, 205
freedom 34, 65, 74, 76, 104, 105, 123, 147
Freud (see also psychoanalysis) 10, 64, 69, 74, 112, 159

gender
    boys 25, 35, 40, 54, 70, 79, 124, 142
    girls 25, 42, 46, 79, 181, 187
    men 71, 75, 78, 99, 100, 125, 181, 185
    women 6, 17, 71, 82, 90, 96, 97, 99, 100, 183, 194, 209
ghost (also phantom, shade, ghoul, spectre) 10, 22, 24, 25, 28, 69, 73, 74, 78, 124, 213, 214
Golden section 44, 45, 47, 49, 50, 51, 117
Greenstone 7, 8, 15, 72, 79, 80, 87, 93, 108, 129, 140

Hall, David 90, 92, 93
Harris, Walter 72, 120

Hastings 13, 98, 113, 187, 189, 190, 191
headmaster (also principal) 13, 55, 56, 71, 162, 164, 174, 180, 195
Henderson
    Keith 12, 13, 62, 73, 75, 162, 174, 179, 203, 204, 205, 207
    Elliot 11, 12, 179
Here and Now 26, 115, 116, 117, 118, 120, 121, 128
Hood, Lynley 7, 8, 10, 11, 14, 19, 72, 89, 90, 91, 94, 118, 119, 138, 188, 197, 199, 214
Horoera 12, 73, 74, 202
Hyde, Robin 91, 39

I Passed This Way 5, 7, 13, 14, 87, 92, 96, 113, 118, 119, 123, 129, 139, 183, 184, 194
Incense to Idols 6, 7, 11, 85, 87, 88, 91, 92, 97, 98, 100, 103, 104, 107, 108, 129, 133, 183, 191, 193
infants 49, 122, 176
    infant methods 71
    infant room 15, 20, 26, 27, 28, 32, 33, 37, 39, 42, 45, 48, 49, 51, 53, 54, 55, 56, 59, 68, 69, 71, 84, 93, 116, 117, 126, 147, 187, 188, 201
    infant teacher 72
inservice courses 66, 70
inspectors of schools 63
Isaacs, Susan 66, 122, 124, 128

Japanese 74, 182

Kraus, Lili 120

Landfall 92, 97, 99, 103
letters (see also correspondence) 44, 72, 77, 132, 134, 139, 141, 146, 193, 199, 204, 206, 208, 210
Lewis, Roland 72, 118, 125
Listener (also *New Zealand Listener*) 92, 96, 97, 113, 121, 198
London 13, 76, 142, 193, 204, 205

McConaghy, Cathryn 8, 9, 79
McEldowney, Dennis 89, 91, 93, 109

Māori
    arts and crafts 67, 70, 94
    children 10, 11, 20, 37, 67, 69, 79, 82, 86, 93, 94, 115, 116, 119, 121, 124, 164, 167, 188, 201
    culture 70, 80, 93, 94, 124, 186, 187
    language 11, 68, 77, 80, 164, 169, 175, 176
    mythology 64, 68
    teachers 11, 165
Māori Schools/ Native Schools 10, 13, 14, 15, 16, 65, 67, 68, 70, 71, 72, 81, 82, 83, 84, 120, 169
May, Helen 66
Moeke-Maxwell, Tess 8, 80
mother/motherhood 11, 12, 21, 24, 27, 66, 73, 76, 77, 104, 125, 141, 180, 181, 184, 198, 213
music
    piano 80, 100, 102, 120, 123, 124, 147, 150, 163, 164, 173, 187, 190, 201, 203, 204
    songs/ singing 24, 26, 48, 49, 50, 70, 150, 186, 190, 206
Myself 7, 13, 14, 62, 64, 72, 73, 74, 75, 87, 95, 129, 182, 183

National Education 10, 11, 19, 20, 26, 32, 37, 42, 44, 51, 55, 69, 115, 117, 118, 119, 120, 121, 122, 137
native imagery 16, 147, 152, 158
nature study 44, 45, 50, 51, 117, 150
nervous breakdown 13, 24, 69, 74
New Education (see also Progressive Education) 64, 66, 67, 70, 72, 73, 77
    New Education Fellowship (NEF) 65
    New Education Fellowship (NEF) Conference, 1937 66, 124
New Era 65
New York 12, 13, 76, 129, 133, 134, 137, 141, 146, 204, 205, 206, 207
New York Times 6, 132, 135, 136
New Zealand
    Book Award 96
    Educational Institute (NZEI) 10,19, 69, 115, 116, 119, 120, 121

publishers 9, 118
society, culture and character 20,42, 43, 62, 64, 65, 67, 68,70, 79, 80, 90, 93, 94, 96, 99, 100, 103, 105, 107, 116, 122, 124, 186, 187
woollen curtain 101, 132, 133, 138
Ngata, Sir Apirana 56, 70, 72, 175
number/numeracy 16, 44, 45, 46, 47, 49, 50, 51, 117, 128, 174

organic
    reading 20, 37, 39, 40, 42, 43, 44, 116, 120, 152
    teaching 42, 51, 52, 53, 84, 116, 117, 119, 137
    writing 32, 34, 35, 36, 37, 41, 117

pā 34, 35, 38, 53, 56, 57, 79, 114, 201
piano (see music)
Pipiriki 13, 62, 64, 72, 73, 74, 80, 94, 123, 180, 181, 182, 183, 184, 202
poetry 64, 70, 77, 110, 136, 158, 212
principal (see also headmaster) 123
Progressive Education (see also New Education) 61, 62, 64, 122, 172
Provocations 8
psychic 9, 51, 69, 79
psychoanalysis 64, 125
    psychoanalytic theory 13, 115, 124
psychology 64, 71, 146, 154, 159
publishers 9, 88, 90, 118, 146, 205
    Heinemann 137
    Knopf 7, 12, 14, 108, 141, 143
    New Zealand publishing 9, 118
    Simon and Schuster 12, 131, 132, 141

race 37, 42, 53, 62, 67, 68, 70, 79, 80
reading 8, 10, 20, 21, 24, 25, 26, 27, 29, 30, 33, 34, 37, 38, 39, 40, 41, 42, 43, 44, 52, 53, 59, 63, 64, 65, 68, 69, 77, 113, 114, 115, 116, 117, 119, 120, 136, 150, 152, 153, 156, 188, 198, 201, 203, 206
    creative reading scheme 21
    Ihaka books 113, 188

key vocabulary 10, 20, 21, 25, 26, 27, 28, 29, 32, 37, 74, 114, 116, 117, 118, 119, 121, 122, 150, 152, 153, 154, 156, 202, 210
   key words 25, 27, 32, 69, 79, 80, 113, 122
   literacy 10, 116, 159
   transitional readers 113, 117
romantic/romanticism 93, 140
Rhodes, Winston 88, 93, 94
rhythm 148, 150, 153, 154, 207, 211

Selah 78, 181, 182, 185, 188, 202
Sex
   kiss 10, 25, 28, 69
   love 25, 26, 28, 93, 94, 113, 118, 124, 131, 134, 142, 168, 180, 183, 185, 189, 210
   sex words (key vocabulary) 25
Simon, Judith 10, 62, 72, 169
Smith, Linda Tuhiwai 10, 62, 72, 169
Somerset, Joy (née Alley) (see also Alley, Joy.)
Spearpoint 7, 13, 87, 129, 146
Spinster 6, 7, 10, 13, 86, 87, 88, 89, 90, 91, 92, 93, 94, 104, 107, 108, 124, 130, 131, 132, 133, 134, 153, 154, 159, 188, 192, 200, 201, 205, 209, 212
Stead, C. K. 6, 12, 86, 89, 95, 96, 97, 129
Stevens, Joan 86, 88, 91, 93, 97, 100, 192
Stories from the River 96

Tauranga 13, 14 ,192, 194, 198, 199, 204
Teacher 6, 7, 10, 11, 12, 13, 14, 64, 65, 69, 70, 72, 73, 86, 87, 92, 93, 94, 108, 111, 117, 118, 119, 120, 121, 122, 125, 129, 131, 134, 137, 142, 146, 153, 158, 201, 202, 209, 210
television 5, 7, 78
Three 7, 13, 87, 88, 96, 107, 129, 131, 140, 183, 193
Time magazine 91, 132, 192
tone 55, 56, 57, 93, 95, 117

violence 10, 74, 75, 105

Waiomatatini 11, 13, 120, 161, 162–164, 171, 172, 176, 184, 185, 186, 202
war
   First World War 65, 66, 73, 186
   Second World War 62, 65, 73, 80, 186
Whanganui River 13, 73
Whenua 86
Woolf, Virginia 76, 78
writer/writing 6, 7, 8, 10, 11, 13, 24, 31, 32, 33, 34, 35, 36, 37, 38, 39, 40, 47, 52, 62, 63, 66, 73, 76, 77, 78, 86, 87, 88, 89, 90, 91, 92, 93, 94, 95, 96, 97, 104, 105, 106, 107, 108, 110, 112, 113, 114, 117, 118, 119, 120, 122, 123, 131, 133, 138, 139, 140, 141, 151, 152, 155, 158, 180, 183, 197, 198, 202, 203, 207, 209, 214

www.ingramcontent.com/pod-product-compliance
Lightning Source LLC
Chambersburg PA
CBHW081330230426
43667CB00018B/2882